DAYS of '41

DAYS

BY ED SHEEHAN

of '41

Pearl Harbor Remembered

KAPA ASSOCIATES, LTD.
Honolulu

The watercolor sketch used for the front cover was executed by Myles
Tanaka; the photograph of the author on the back cover was taken by
Gisela Johnson.

For Sally, again

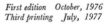

First edition   October, 1976
Third printing   July, 1977

Published by Kapa Associates, Ltd., 677 Ala Moana Boulevard, Honolulu,
Hawaii 96813. Protected by copyright under terms of the International
Copyright Union; all rights reserved. Printed and first published in Japan.

ISBN 0-915870-01-0   LCC Card No. 76-28601

TABLE OF CONTENTS

PREFACE

Two large squadrons of Japanese planes appeared in the skies north of Oahu, Hawaii, on the morning of December 7th in 1941. They were totally unexpected.

The surprise-attack plan, masterminded by Admiral Isoroku Yamamoto, worked perfectly. At 7:55 a.m. the planes were roaring down to maim and destroy major ships of the United States Pacific Fleet at Pearl Harbor. In the time you will use to read this page over a thousand men were killed.

And a thousand heroes were born.

Very ordinary men did most extraordinary things. They lifted objects it was thought impossible to lift, moved with broken backs, walked with feet shot off and serviced guns with fractured arms. Some fought on at battle stations knowing they would drown. Others swam to rescue comrades in flaming oil. Messmen manned guns, musicians steered boats, machinists tied tourniquets and nurses hauled lines. Eight U.S. battleships, three cruisers, three destroyers and eight other craft were sunk or badly damaged. Almost half of America's combat aircraft on Oahu were destroyed. In one hour and fifty minutes, ships and air forces of United States' power in the Pacific were brutally crippled.

Final toll was 1,143 wounded and 2,341 Americans killed.

A special world in Hawaii also died that morning. I was a young man then who lived in Waikiki and worked at Pearl Harbor. This book is an effort to recall that time and the way it was on the island of Oahu.

The changes since have been enormous.

The somnolent, 1941 port of Honolulu is now a rich and dynamic Pacific capital, nourished by United States and international interests and dominated by a home-grown multiracial business and social leadership. After Pearl Harbor, Hawaii's young men of all races went off to fight and die in every war theater on the globe. Island Americans of Japanese ancestry formed what became the most decorated unit in the U.S. Army, and when they and their fellow warriors returned, scarred and wiser, there was no place in their futures for old ways of control by sugar and pineapple planters. The war fed the seeds of change; Statehood brought them to flower. Hawaii now has both a governor and U.S. senator of Japanese ancestry. Both soldiered with honor, and the senator left his right arm in Italy.

From the sea today, Waikiki is a jagged cliff of hotels stacked along a world-famous beach. Fleets of taxis and limousines now service concrete colossi where the small cottages, cafes and shops of 1941 once stood. The flowered little lanes have long been streets, walled in by towers and punctuated by traffic lights. An oldtimer, on a sentimental stroll through the hamlet treasured in memory can become quite confused.

Happily, many important things remain unchanged.

A remarkable benevolence must be presiding over these most isolated bits of land on earth. Mornings rise in beauty, and days flow along with minimum abrasions upon the spirit. The sky is a crisp blue, and violet-tinted balls of cumulus pause upon the blunted peaks of the windward mountains. Tradewinds still riffle the emerald shallows at Kuhio Beach, and its big banyan tree throws even wider shade on dozing retirees. Island women of all races grow lovelier, and island children are becoming more beautiful blends of East and West than were ever seen before. In the pasteled twilight along Kalakaua Avenue, a new generation of old men grouses over cribbage hands on benches above the sand. Another generation watches and waits.

The focal point for a tour of Pearl Harbor today is the *Arizona* memorial.

The 184-foot structure in purest white resembles a ship's bridge standing astride the remains of the sunken battleship. Its center section is unwalled, and visitors can

The USS Arizona *Memorial at Pearl Harbor
as it is today. United States Navy Official Photo.*

look over the rails at the barnacled remnants and weed-covered gunmounts of the ruins beneath the water. Farther out, at either side of the memorial, markers indicate the ship's bow and stern. Colorful small fish flit in and out of openings in the hulk. Just the other day one of the mushroom-shaped ventilators that had been protruding out of the water for all these years, finally rusted away and toppled. Surprisingly, beads of oil still seep up from the ship's bowels thirty-five years after she was sunk, making an iridescent film upon the calm surface of the water.

One end of the memorial forms a chapel-like chamber. A wall here bears the names of the *Arizona's* 1,177 men who died aboard her that morning, and whose bodies were left entombed in their ship. The navy honors them by raising and lowering the nation's colors every day, with appropriate ceremony.

The nearby shore of Ford Island is scrub-covered and quiet. Living quarters can be seen under clusters of coconut palms and tall spears of pine trees. Farther, big boxlike hangars loom, without life. Unused seaplane ramps slanting into the bay are bordered by weeds. Landing fields on the island are employed now for small-plane traffic—and little of that. On the Middle Loch side, the cadaver of the battleship *Utah* rests in shallows, like a beached leviathan. In the distance, mothballed navy craft are lashed together, gray and forlorn, seeming to exist only on a list somewhere.

Inland, heavy traffic swarms constantly past naval housing, speeding along overpasses of an expanding freeway system. Thousands of roofs now checker what were once the sugar lands of Aiea and high rises slash against the soft curves of the hills above. The closer view inshore from the memorial shows the big silent buildings of the supply center, a small grove of masts in a yacht anchorage, and the Ford Island ferry on its plodding journey.

Faint sounds of metal being worked and flashes from welder's arcs come across the water from the submarine base and shipyard repair basin. Except for these insinuations of continuing life, what was once Battleship Row is curiously quiet. Thick concrete moorings that secured the doomed ships in 1941 jut out of water like a row of tombstones. In sunshine, the *Arizona* memorial blazes white.

The big tour boats come daily and their viewing decks are always crowded. Most trips begin in Honolulu with an almost festive air. A million people each year take the tour, most of whom were not born at the time of the attack. For many, the excursion is part of a prepurchased vacation package. Dress is casual, although some clients must be advised that bikinis are not in good taste. Visitors run the spectrum of nationalities, and include many Japanese, invariably silent and respectful. Boat operators say that very few veterans of the attack come these days, or, if they do, choose not to identify themselves. One boat captain told me that often he could tell a survivor of the attack from other tourists. "They have a special look," he said, "and they're always the very quiet ones."

One such passenger came in 1965. He was Kazuo Sakamaki, the only survivor of the crews assigned to five midget submarines Japan sent against the harbor. He wrote of the visit later: "I was all alone, the others were all Americans. I did not speak to anyone. No one in the group of sightseers knew who I was. I was attacked by strange impressions."

As the boat guide's narration drones on, conversation trickles into silence and faces become serious. Always, a remarkable transformation occurs in the passengers: the outing ceases to be a Tour and becomes a Pilgrimage. The litany of devastation and death is delivered with the unwitting monotony of a tale retold a thousand times: "Over two thousand men were killed here

11

in less than two hours . . . . ''

Tradewinds soothe, sunlight sparkles on the water, the silence becomes complete.

Even without the recital, Pearl Harbor holds a haunting sadness. Once, these quiet lagoons were the setting for the most tragic hour in American history. The sorrow lingers in the soft air, arrested here for all time on that Sunday morning when a world was changed. Surely, centuries from now, even on a day with the sun high and the eternal mountains at peace, people who come here will know that this is a place where something terrible happened.

●　●　●　●　●　●　●　●　●

No single account can possibly cover all the events leading up to the attack on Pearl Harbor. The thick volumes of the Congressional hearings *alone* fill almost three feet on a library shelf. Interested readers will find fascinating accounts in Walter Lord's *Day of Infamy* and Gordon Prange's *Tora, Tora, Tora!* Roberta Wohlstetter's *Pearl Harbor, Warning and Decision,* is a remarkable study of the communications and intelligence aspects of the subject. Captain Homer Wallin's *Pearl Harbor, Why, How, Fleet Salvage and Appraisal,* is a mine of detail about the colossal job of salvage done after December 7th, and also contains rare, first-person accounts of the day by survivors. The *Honolulu Advertiser* and *Honolulu Star Bulletin* libraries contain engrossing material, including Buck Buchwach's reports titled "Japan Visit" in May of 1969. Sections of the present work were published on December 4, 1966, in the combined Sunday edition of the *Advertiser* and the *Star-Bulletin,* and, in rather different form, a portion was published as a book in 1971 under the title *One Sunday Morning.*

DAYS of '41

PART ONE

PLANTINGS

"Within ten miles of our city lies a magnificent sheet of water known as Pearl Harbor, securely protected from the ocean and presenting no less than eighteen miles of water frontage.... Ships of the largest size can moor alongside or moor the shore and be perfectly secure in the severest storms....

"This unrivalled harbor has evidently been designed by a wise creator for some great purpose...."

—Henry Whitney
Editor, *The Hawaiian Gazette*
Honolulu, 1873

On a map of Oahu, Pearl Harbor is shaped like a spreading tree, its outline enclosing some eight square miles of landlocked water near Honolulu. Ford Island lies near its center and a winding channel connects the inner reaches with the sea. Three large areas of water are known as East, Middle and West Lochs, the latter word being a legacy from Scotsmen who surveyed the area.

For many centuries before the white man came, only canoes of Hawaiians floated over Wai Momi, or Pearl Water. Then in 1793, Britain's George Vancouver, seeking sweet water for his crews, sent men to investigate a report of a "channel capable of sheltering large ships." They returned with the information that Wai Momi did, indeed, have several spacious bays, but that the presence of a coral reef and sand obstructions at the entrance "renders it fit only for reception of very small craft."

Another hundred years passed and more, and still there was little activity along the shores of Pearl Harbor. Winds moving down from the Koolau Mountains and the central plain of Oahu feathered the water in miles of calm lagoon. Torch fishermen waded in its shallows at night and others drew mullet nets by day. Taro was grown in marshy patches inland near Aiea, and sugar cane waved on higher ground. A scattering of Hawaiians lived along the shores among groves of coconut, milo and kiawe trees and life went on quietly, as it had in ancient times.

America acquired the Hawaiian Islands by annexation in 1898—and with them the advantages that a naval base at Pearl Harbor would offer. By 1903, Navy authorities were preparing to dredge open the reef to make an entrance into the harbor. As the year ended, engineers on the job finally took a small launch into the broad lochs, the first craft flying the U.S. flag to enter Pearl Harbor.

Its name was *Dirty Kate* and there is no record of any ceremony to mark the occasion.

The Navy's engineers who dredged Pearl Harbor's entrance at the turn of the century respected the old beliefs of the Hawaiians. Those beliefs were important, for the spirit-guardians of many Hawaiians took the form of a shark. And the eastern side of the Pearl Harbor area, called Puuloa, was a most sacred place, because the great shark demi-goddess, Kaapuhau, dwelled there.

Therefore, early diggers heeded warnings that Kaapuhau might take vengeance for any defiling of her residence. The proper kind of kahuna, or priest, was summoned from among the experts in the artistic and spiritual lore of Hawaii. He conducted the appropriate ceremonies and chanted the necessary prayers. Offerings of fish, pigs and chickens were made to placate the deity.

Stones the ancients believed to be sacred were
gently removed from shallows and buried
reverently at sea. All the right things were done.
And the work was finished without trouble. Clearly,
Kaapuhau was not angry. She did not treat these
haoles, these newcomers, as intruders.

But years later, when another group of
haoles arrived to begin building the important
Drydock Number One, no ceremonies were held
and no priests were consulted. The engineers
bulled right ahead with their digging and
disturbances. To the Hawaiians this could mean
only trouble.

And the trouble came.

It came in 1913 when the great drydock was
almost finished. Pumps thumped day and night to
draw sea water out of the long pit while the last
concrete was being poured into forms. Then,
suddenly one day, workers realized that the dock's
floor was rising beneath them. Whistles shrilled
and men shouted in their frantic efforts to escape.
With a ripping and a cracking sounding like
cannon fire, the dock's floor rose seventeen feet
before it exploded into a million fragments. Water
boiled up through the cracks in furious fountains.
Timbers snapped and were tossed into the air like
toothpicks. The work of four years was undone
in minutes.

Engineering miscalculations, said the
haoles. But the Hawaiians shook their heads,
knowing the true reasons for the destruction.

For two years nothing was done. In 1915,
Congress appropriated one and one half million
dollars to build another drydock. Without it for
ship-repair, Pearl Harbor would never be any-

thing more important than a refueling station in the middle of the vast Pacific.

This time the haoles listened to the Hawaiians. A kahuna was asked to say the prayers and make the sacrifices that would appease Kaapuhau. When at last the drydock was finished, it stood firm. And the first time it was emptied, the corpse of a gigantic shark lay stretched upon its floor.

In 1940, almost a thousand men were recruited from many mainland states to work in the naval shipyard at Pearl Harbor in the Territory of Hawaii. Most were highly skilled journeymen in iron, wood, electric and other construction trades. But many younger ones, including myself, were rated as helpers, presumably because we'd reached a proficiency above that of apprentices and were worthy of hire as assistants to the senior men. In late October we gathered in San Pedro, California, and boarded the SS *Washington* bound for the islands.

The Honolulu of that day was just a sleepy city by the sea, and had never been treated to an influx like ours. Also, the *Washington* was one of the biggest ships ever to touch Honolulu. The newspapers, the day after we landed ran front page stories about our arrival. But on the morning when the big liner eased into its berth in the shadow of Aloha Tower, no one seemed to be expecting us. There were no bands, hula girls or diving boys. Tugs nudged the ship to the dock, we drank in the beauty of the distant mountains, inhaled the aromas of flowers, moist earth and coffee, and waited. Hours passed while red tape was unraveled. When finally we filed ashore trucks were on hand to take us to temporary quarters. We rumbled away through the noontime city. By this time, Honolulu was wide awake.

Through a happy chance, the day was the climax of an election campaign. Hawaiian politics were wonderfully festive in those pretelevision days, and Honolulu's streetcorners were jammed with singers, hula dancers, musicians and speech-making hopefuls. To us haoles from the mainland the scenes were almost unreal, a fantasy of flowers, laughing girls and brown-skinned celebrants, all bathed in bright sunshine. The introduction was perfect, like a preview of pleasures and discoveries to come.

Within a matter of weeks, hundreds of us younger men were drawn to Waikiki, for the same reason people are today—it's the place where you can have the most fun. Rentals were low for small bungalows and apartments, the beach was a few yards distant, and the life style was uninhibited and easy.

Only three miles from downtown Honolulu, Waikiki was synonymous with the Hawaii of travel posters, Harry Owens's songs and the standard daydream of life on a tropic isle. It had scant commerce, no office buildings or docks and was neat and quiet, a village sort of place. Going barefoot was its way of life and smiles were always in fashion. In daytime it was drowned in brilliant sun, and in the night, relaxed and langorous under a sparkling dust of stars.

You can hardly see the Royal Hawaiian Hotel now, dwarfed as it is among extravagant

risings of newer complexes, but it was then a
splendid, pink, Moorish pile dominating the whole
shore. Acres of bright green lawns and beds of
plants on the street side provided pleasant places
to sit on benches under soaring coco palms. Other
hotels nearby were the mansionlike Moana and the
gracious cluster of bungalows at the Halekulani.
The strip of sand fronting these hotels was never
crowded, not even on weekends. The only other
buildings of any size along Kalakaua Avenue were
the Waikiki Theater and a low, modest branch of
a downtown department store. The Moana Hotel
was also landlord of a grouping of neat white
cottages across the street, roughly where the
International Market Place now sprawls. Where
the Princess Kaiulani Hotel now towers was a dank
and jungly sort of greenhouse area that supplied
the Royal and Moana with flowers and potted
plants. Kalakaua Avenue in 1940 was only spottily
mercantile and dozens of private homes still faced
the uncrowded road. Very few structures were
more than three stories tall and there were many
vacant lots, patches of lawn and even small palm
groves along the beach boulevard. Neighborhood
side streets were narrow and many curbless. Some
were unpaved, gravelly lanes. Not a single traffic
light scarred Waikiki in 1940. There was no need
for one; a citizen could stroll quite safely across
any street, at any time of day or night, giving
complete attention to a newspaper.

   Almost every cottage in Waikiki sat amid
lush greenery, under coconut, monkeypot, mango
or banyan trees. Panax hedges or flowering
bushes served as token fences. Flowers grew as if
uncontrollable: plumeria of rich and heavy scent,

velvety hibiscus in warm colors, and bougainvillea flaming like sunsets in orange, red and purple. Even at the height of its activity Waikiki was a place dozing in tropical brilliance, a broad strand of comfortable homes inhabited by people who moved unhurriedly and smiled easily. Overwhelmingly, one's neighbors were generous, kind and trusting. Waikikians rarely locked their doors then. You simply left the house, and came back hours, even days later, to find everything just as you had left it.

We who were in our early twenties in 1940 had been teenagers during the Great Depression. Almost all my contemporaries at Pearl Harbor had been reared in pinchpenny harshness, knowing the unending struggles of fathers, families and friends. My own background near Boston was typical: high school dropout, day-laborer, tree-trimmer, stockbroker's messenger and helping my father with sheet-metal jobs when he could find work. My top pay had been $18 a week, and most of that went without question to help feed our family.

Suddenly, in Hawaii, those years of denial were left far behind. For lads like me the jobs at Pearl meant the best pay we'd ever had. There was money in our pockets, even as much as a spare twenty-dollar bill now and then. We indulged our whims in food, drink, books and clothes. Time was not the only thing to be spent recklessly. All our currencies seemed to be in limitless supply.

In the drift that hundreds of us made to Waikiki we found new friends easily and quickly.

The alliances warmed and ripened. We shared a drunkenness of the spirit in the startling release to tropic softness. And Hawaii was a wonderful place in which to be young.

Mornings are remembered best, when Waikiki came alive in many little arousings.

Night cool dissipated as the sun crept over the mountains. If the tide was high, waves slapped gently against the Kuhio Beach seawall. Early hunting seabirds fluttered like snowflakes in first slants of light. A few swimmers and surfers emerged from hotels and were soon tiny figures on tumbling crests far out. Across from the banyan tree at Kuhio Beach, tentative rustlings of commerce began at the gas station and the drug store. A curbside cab driver or two yawned his way out of cramped sleep. And usually there was the rumpled form of a sailor or soldier sleeping off an overdose of liberty on one of the beachside benches. Shopkeepers along Kalakaua unhooked doors and hosed down sidewalks. A few cars muttered along the beach road from the Kahala, Kapahulu and Diamond Head areas. There was the clink of ice and milk being delivered to the Aoki grocery and the lady barbers a few doors away mopped floors and polished mirrors. In sidestreets, newsboys aimed their folded missives over flowers toward front porches. Housewives opened windows wide for sunshine and tradewinds. Raucous mynah-bird congresses clamored in trees. The morning sun arched up over softness, muffled news on the radio, sounds of breakfasts, whispers of surf, scents of seaweed and brine.

Other things happened in their own time. Residents straggled off to jobs in downtown

Honolulu. Beachboys corralled tourist clients for surfing lessons and canoe rides. One or two foot patrolmen ambled along the avenue and found nothing awry. And every morning, older men began sauntering down sidestreets to gather under arbors of hau trees by the sea. There they sat, to talk and play cribbage through the day and into the dark. The games were interrupted only by sleeping time.

Almost all the card players were retired soldiers and sailors, and their loyalties remained fierce. They traded insults at the slightest provocation, but under the veneer of gruffness was a nagging nostalgia for Older Days, Better Times, and The Way Things Used To Be . . . The sailors recalled China Duty, the Japanese shelling of the gunboat *Panay* on the Yangstze, how it was to live like a prince in Shanghai on a seaman's pay—and of the time when a certain President's wife questioned whether American sailors who had wallowed in Oriental lechery were fit to associate with nice American girls on their return to the States.

And the soldiers reminisced about the Old Army and how tough it was, of the spit and polish and comradeship found in barracks life, and of doing hard time in the Schofield stockade on "piss and punk," as they called the jail fare of bread and water. They orated about how much better Honolulu was before the crowds of newcomers arrived. And they bemoaned the softness of the new breed of soldiers, those skinny, snot-nosed kids who were ashamed to wear their uniforms in town. There was no respect or pride any more, by Christ. Why, in the old days a man would spend all morning shining his leather . . .

The ramblings of the cribbage players went on and on. Their games were forums for the past, hooks on which the castoff warriors hung their days. Listening to them was the first time I remember thinking about how it would be to grow old.

Long before the Kuhio Beach cribbage players began reprising their more vigorous days, we Pearl Harbor workers would be up and on the move. The girls at the Unique Lunch would be preparing lomi-salmon and purplish poi for Hawaiian food lovers, the Blue Ocean Cafe would have admitted its first supplicants for a hair of the dog, and we would be ensconced on stools at the Benson Smith Drug Co., Ltd.

This was our favorite morning oasis, a small and quite ordinary drugstore with the standard miscellany of potions, pills, notions and beach gear. For us, its principal attactions were the pretty, blackhaired Japanese waitresses who worked at its lunch counter with fetching femininity. The windows opened upon Kalakaua Avenue and the Waikiki Tavern across the street, and we could sit, flirt with the girls, inspect the early strollers and watch the neighborhood fuss to life. We all knew each other and the morning's pause was a ritual of competing for the waitresses' attentions over sweet chilled papaya and aromatic Kona coffee.

Several of us waited there daily for Captain Ernie to arrive with our transport to Pearl. Ernie was a rigger boss and, like other canny senior men, stuffed his car with younger commuters who paid a weekly fee for the service. Captain Ernie's own breakfast was a four ounce dollop of neat bourbon, ingested while he donned his uniform of starched khaki. Since boyhood he had spent his life on sailing ships and he had no small talk. He would stride to the drugstore's door, face flushed and glowering, and bawl: "O.K. you friggin' swabs. I'm shovin' off!"

We bolted our food and *went*. His was a bosun's bellow, daring disobedience, implying indescribable punishment for lingerers. The little waitresses winced and an occasional browsing tourist recoiled in fear from those blasts. But now, looking back, I think Ernie's swashbuckling summons was the loudest noise we ever heard in Waikiki before the war.

The narrow road from Honolulu to Pearl Harbor in early 1941 ran for a couple of miles through sugarcane fields. Along the route, travelers also went over the Keehi Lagoon marshes and passed a few rickety stores and houses near where Honolulu International Airport now stands. Just before Pearl, the Hickam Field gate was on the left.

Pearl Harbor's main gate then was little more than an opening in the fence at the end of the road. A small wooden reception shack squatted nearby and the Marine Barracks and Navy Receiving Station were a stone's throw inside. Marines who pulled guard duty at the gate took shelter in a pyramidal tent near the entrance.

The harbor was about two minutes' drive farther in, and shops of different crafts were lined facing Drydock One. The dock was empty that first day I went to Pearl and I remember how huge it seemed, a great concrete container carved out of the earth. Ten-Ten Dock, a long stretch of pier, ran straight down the shore. To the west, across several hundred yards of water, flat Ford Island sat with its clumps of trees stuck off on the sides. The island's hangars and airstrips, which covered most of its surface, were quiet. A few seaplanes sat on runways slanting into the water. Several warships were resting at moorings along the shore. Two or three launches and double-ended small boats putted about on the calm. Inland shores were quiet. Far hillsides sloped up in patches of green and copper to mountains blue in the sun.

The first impression was of spaciousness, then of how sunny and peaceful the scene was in the gentle air. Almost always before, while I was learning the tin-knockers' trade with my father, we had labored in cramped places, usually cellars, wet-dirty and dark. I had never liked the work and everything I learned had been absorbed reluctantly. But I felt that first day at Pearl Harbor, that somehow the occupation might be different in Hawaii, much more pleasant. As time moved on, quite often it was.

Shop 17, the tin-roofed headquarters of the metal trades, was one of the battered structures whose fronts faced on Drydock One. It was a cavernous place of crashing din in sooty twilight. Hammers banged and machinery clattered constantly. A foundry occupied one section, and when molten steel was poured there, workers nearby made a wild scramble to escape the hellish heat and

showers of burning metallic rain. The shop had
no flooring in many places, only dirt packed as
hard as stone. In the rear, a corner had been cleared
for a few bruised benches and dented lockers.
Between shifts, this was our spot for socializing.

At first the local men treated us with sullen
reserve. The shock of many hundreds of new faces
suddenly appearing in their small shipyard-
community piqued curiosity and suspicion. Both
these sentiments were returned. Few of us
mainlanders had known Hawaiians, Chinese,
Portuguese, Filipinos—or any of their mixtures—
before. We found their pidgin English baffling and
their foods—like raw fish, poi, cold rice and strange
sausages—highly suspect. But as weeks and then
months passed, a rapport was slowly established
and acquaintances became friends, both on and
off the job.

Within its sprawl, Pearl Harbor in 1941
held many kinds of men: fumblers, grumblers,
proud artisans and utter incompetents. Some of
us were men in waning vitality, others stood at its
youthful height. Sailors, marines, civilians, we
were the all-knowing young and the tiring old,
and, as well, micks, bohunks, hebes, squareheads
and dagos. We used such slurring words casually
and without rancor, as illusions and prejudices
diminished in our comradeship. We had come from
farms and alleys, city canyons and small town
mainstreets. Rednecks, prairie men, hillbillies and
city dwellers, we were all suddenly the same—
strangers, thrown together in a harbor, on an
island, in the middle of the world's greatest
ocean.

Off the job we splintered into groups of

many interests. To those my age, in early twenties, these were sun and surf, macho boasting, swing music, and girls. The island wahines were a delight then as they are now, and we took great pleasure in the tawniness of Hawaiians, the goldenness of sun-dyed Orientals, the Latin lushness of Portuguese and the delicate litheness of fine boned Filipinas. But sadly, our numbers over-whelmed theirs, particularly in the Waikiki area. An enormous amount of effort was expended in trying to bed these multiracial lovelies, but few of us managed to get even a date. Haole girls were scarcer, cool and clannish, sheltering within the strictures of a provincial white society.

So we did the best we could and, when we failed, made do with the best the days could offer and savored spendthrift nights. When not engaged in the mating dances we drank beer, read a bit and bragged clumsily, hinting at great deeds still undone and virgins facing deflowering. Our older companions listened and chuckled their scorn, returning to their newspapers, debates about baseball or card games for penny stakes. The Great Depression had planted caution deep in most of them, worn them down into dry and dour figures. Virtually all had wives and children on the main-land. Grudgingly, they would admit that Hawaii was pretty, the sun mighty nice and the work O.K. But the Hard Times just past seemed to have been tattooed on their senses and their days led only to the bank or postal savings. Overtime pay was a preferred substitute for wasteful pleasure. For too long their roots had been embedded elsewhere, always their talk turned to home. To us younger men the Depression decade was a blessedly fading memory. There was so much time ahead . . . In that time, in that place, it seemed that nothing unfortunate could ever happen again.

In that summer of 1941, lawns were like billiard table tops and hedges were crewcut in front of the 14th Naval District headquarters at Pearl Harbor. Officers and men wore snowy whites and bright flags of country and command rippled above the long lanais.

Not far away was the Yard Cafeteria, a large, one-room building set with picnic-type tables and decorated with safety posters, a bulletin board and a garish juke box. The Honolulu entrepreneur who ran this monopoly served terrible food and was the only enemy we unanimously identified.

Looking north inland, a littered field lay between the cafeteria and docks of the repair basin. A marine railway on which smaller ships were drawn out of the water stood at one end of the line of docks, looking like an abandoned erector-set construction. The basin's piers were concrete fingers poking into stretches of East Loch, and on one a huge stationary hammerhead crane, painted in large checks, swung high over masts of ships often moored below. The blunt, wedge-shape of the hammerhead is still Pearl Harbor's most distinctive structure, decorated now in a Hawaiian tapa-cloth motif by whimsical workmen.

Most of Pearl's shipyard activity took place in the repair basin. From its piers you could gaze across the channel at the flat platter of Ford Island or a few supply sheds on Kuahua Peninsula. A turn to your right gave a view of the submarine base beyond a narrow inlet. The towering cylindrical tank where men underwent escape training dominated this scene, and submarines sunned their black backs like dolphins in a calm, as they do today.

Alii Drive curved off along the inland border of the repair basin. "Alii" refers to Hawaii's royalty of old, and the palm-lined street was where high ranking officers lived. The officers' club and tennis courts also adjoined the repair basin.

Except for Ford Island, aloof beyond its broad moat, everything then important at Pearl Harbor was within walking distance. White-jacketed messmen served drinks, yardmen in fatigues scissored grass, and heartless slot machines coughed coins only short distances from where workmen slipped into pitch dark tanks of submarines or convoluted depths of destroyers. Workers boiled tar and riveters ripped the air within a pebble's toss of the admirals' offices. The noises and flames of ship repair rose not far from the bright lawns and quiet old houses of the naval alii. Farther along the shore, miles of Pearl's coastline held nothing but kiawe scrub and dusty weeds. A few old shacks drooped under the feathery trees, and taro and watercress patches flourished in low places beyond the shore highway. Youngsters from plantation camps splashed in the harbor's shallows, and soon after dawn every day, tuna sampans murmured in to net their nehu-baitfish. Inland from the harbor, gentle slopes led one's eyes up to the smokestacks of the sugar mill at Aiea, and to fields of tall cane waving tassels in the breeze.

I enjoyed a full-fledged helper rating at Pearl Harbor, but no lines were formed or bids made for my services.

There was a great deal I did not know about sheet-metal work, despite the years of grudged apprenticeship to my patient father. I drifted from one journeyman-boss to another, getting by, then met my nemesis when assigned to an Oklahoman called Shep. Old Shep (he was at least fifty) was stone dry of patience on the job. A dedicated craftsman, he approached his work with the seriousness of a brain surgeon. With his head and shoulders hidden in a compartment, he would thrust his hand back and I was expected to slap the proper tool in working position into that hand immediately. Failing, as I often did, I would then have to endure a tongue lashing that could be heard at great distances: "Dumb goddam Yankee . . . you don't know yore *ass* from a ball-peen hammer . . . " On he railed while I cringed, face aflame.

Shep terrified me, but it was all for the good. By the end of some five months I had suffered through a first rate cram-course in marine tin-knocking and moved instinctively on tiptoes in the presence of my superiors.

Then he left. The decision to go had been brewing for some time. He didn't like Hawaiians— or any other dark folks for that matter. Or the weather, which was too goddam hot, or the food, which was downright heathen with all them rice balls, funny fish and "liberry" paste. And he missed his family. I'm sure it was the last reason that really caused him to leave.

I watched him go with a mixture of

sadness and relief. Near the end he had become
almost kindly, frequently warning me about
throwing money away and "keepin' company with
them native women." Our parting was brief. A day
came when he packed his tools, said things were
better now in Tulsa and he was going home. He
was gone the next day.

Many other faces and voices of the time
have never left me.

Sammy Morgan had learned his iron-
worker's trade as a boy in Scotland's Clydeside
shipyards. Sammy's Gaelic burr was a rippling tune.
He wore rimless glasses over Santa Claus cheeks
and came merrily to work daily with a hint of
whiskey on his breath.

Sailor Jerry, another shipfitter, was a
tattoo artist in off hours. Jerry was fond of discuss-
ing his dream of sailing a small sloop around the
world in the company of two beautiful young
girls. He specified that they would be Chinese,
virgins (for starters) and would remain nude at all
times. "One for eatin' and one for screwin',"
Jerry explained.

Another harmless monomaniac was
Chalmers, a welder obsessed by his bagpipes. At
the request of his Waikiki neighbors (firmly
transmitted by the police), he was forced to hold
his practice sessions in the center of Kapiolani
Park. I can see and hear him now, a tiny figure on
the turf, sending martial wailings out into
the twilight.

And other good companions of the days
and nights: Jimmy Jones, a Virginian of gentle
manner and warming smile; burly and bearded
Jack Copess, a connoisseur of fine wines, leather

and tools; Howard Shanley, goodnaturedly suffering mimicry of his Brooklyn accent, and Johnny Mayernick, an armwaving debater, always eager to take the offensive on any subject.

We were all readers, but Big Bill Lorenz was the most bookish. He carried and caressed books, seemed forever poised to take intellectual leaps. Bud Friedlander was another scholar and muser, a jazz fan with a cool veneer over great warmth. He was the only college man in our group and had brought his patrician-lovely wife to Honolulu. These two accomplishments endowed him with advanced status as a genuine sophisticate.

My closest friend was Gorman Noland, a toolmaker trained in the Ford plant at Dearborn. We struck up an acquaintance on the ship and shared the same interests in reading and talk. Before Hawaii his only prospects had been to become a first class machinist and a good union man, living a life revolving around the River Rouge assembly lines. Hawaii was a revelation of bright beauty to him, a promise of freedom in a perennial summer, as it was to me.

From the sea, Waikiki looked like a vast plantation of coconut palms, with a sprinkle of hotels and cottages spilling out upon the shore. A few cows grazed and hundreds of ducks waddled in marshland where the huge Ala Moana shopping center now rises. Honolulu, a mile or so farther west, was a charming collage of quiet town against a backdrop of valleys and mountains. Aloha Tower, rising 184 feet over the harbor, was the tallest building in all Hawaii in 1941.

Most of the larger buildings downtown clustered in the blocks near the waterfront. Here the business of the Territory was directed: exporting, importing, the buying and selling involving sugar and pineapples, and shipping. On Merchant and Bishop Streets the seasonal cycles of plantations were managed, their harvests recorded, traded and moved. Within a few hundred yards of each other the directors, accountants, lawyers and sea captains kept the commerce of Hawaii in orderly, and, professedly, Christian control.

But only a scant distance from this countinghouse solemnity spread another Honolulu of color, fragrance and noise. And even now, decades later, vivid mental snapshots rise in my memory: plump Hawaiian dowagers stringing flower leis of perfumed brilliance; the manapua man, under his bent yoke with its cans full of the moist delights of Chinese dumplings; the dusky caves of the bars along Hotel Street; Chinatown with its pungent herbshops and posters looking like firecracker labels; the tiny cafes serving Hawaiian delicacies and Oriental noodle specialities . . .

In the Vineyard and River Street area, termite-weakened tenements hugged one another for support. Balconies graced with rococo railings bellied out over narrow alleys. Heavy dark women were framed in upper windows and naked toddlers shrieked at play in the streets. Lines of laundry fluttered everywhere, like ships' pennants hung to dry. Now and then, ancient Chinese matriarchs in splendid brocaded gowns tottered by on bound feet. Gray-haired Japanese ladies wearing fine-figured kimonos glided along on straw slippers.

Hawaiian elders under broad-brimmed lauhala hats strolled with the lonely dignity of those who had once owned the land. And the rejected elders of all races sat on creaky balconies, gazing down ' upon the streetswarm.

In lace-curtained cubicles, up narrow stairs, girls of the Anchor, Rex, Ritz, New Senator and other hookshops slept in, luxuriating after nerve-wracking nights with randy servicemen and civilians. Across Nuuanu Stream, Aala Park was a sanctuary for the lone and lost—winos, beached merchant-ship sailors, assorted dawdlers and cockfight fans. It was also a place where many old men just sat and stared.

Along King Street near the Oahu Railway Depot was a ramshackle maze of dance halls, bars and rooming houses where thousands of Filipinos had congregated. Names here were Cebu Barber, Manila Eats, and Mabuhay Cafe. Nearby, along King, were the Depot Mart and Depot Pawn Shop, along with hardware, fishing tackle and boat gear shops. Displays of Levi's and "Can't Bust 'Em" brand work clothes, plantation goggles, work shirts and service uniforms were heaped on sidewalk tables fronting the swollen stores.

Across the bridge on King Street, the big Oahu Market was a morning babel, rich with smells of roast meat, raw fish, scalded coffee and scented tea. Whole carcasses of shaven pigs hung waxy white on meat hooks. Displayed in row upon row were fruits and vegetables, plucked fowl, cloth bags plump with poi, marbled fishcakes, spice-flecked rice cakes, condiment seaweeds and mottled sausages. Aproned workmen wheeled barrows of bloody fishheads used in making soup.

Junoesque Hawaiian women daintily cubed haupia puddings. Well-dressed Chinese ladies bedecked with fine jade rings haggled over fat pompano and silvery tunas, their bullet-power stilled and stiff. Bare bulbs over the fish stalls dropped raw light on the wet mounds, the multicolored harvests of reefs and blue water.

In Hawaii the sea is everpresent. From earliest days, ships and strangers have built Honolulu and shaped its features and personality. Even the ancients, in mystical prophecy, had called the island Oahu—"the gathering place." On the fringes of town, small houses with neat plantings made pleasant neighborhoods flowing into valleys and clutching hillsides. But in the dense blocks around Honolulu's waterfront, the air was alive with all the pungencies and voices of the Pacific world.

Scarred freighters from far ports gulped holdsful of raw sugar and freshly tinned pineapples. Passenger liners of the Swedes, Germans, British and Japanese delivered a constant trickle of foreign visitors. But it was the Matson fleet out of San Francisco that gave most color to Honolulu's waterfront life. And Boat Day, when the *Lurline* or *Matsonia* arrived off Diamond Head in the early morning sun, meant very special and festive hours in the harbor and the town.

The stirrings and preparations began just before dawn. Lei sellers took favored spots in front of pier sheds and along lower Fort Street, there to sit and chat while stringing garlands chosen from boxes and buckets full of blossoms. The women looked like an arrangement by Gauguin and the thick strands of plumeria, gardenia, ginger, or carnation laced the morning cool with perfume. Then dock workers and a few cops arrived, to begin their bawdy bantering back and forth in Hawaiian. Cab drivers jockeyed for best positions, creating occasional arguments, and the Royal Hawaiian Band's truck unloaded its instruments and chairs. Reporters and photographers arrived to catch the pilot-boat that took them out to the liner for offshore interviews with celebrities. The bartender at the nearby Beaver Grill began polishing glasses at the first crack of light. And when later the crowds of greeters came, the dockside swirled with colors, literally jumped with anticipation.

I can shut my eyes now and smell the flowers, hear the music, feel the lift of excitement as I watch, in memory, the grand white ship being nudged into the inner harbor. Diving boys, looking like seals, bobbed for coins. The air between the ship and pier was bridged with shouts of recognition, and when the ship's deep whistle blew, the concussion could be felt, a blast filling every corner, pronouncing that another journey was ended, that it was time now for greeting and aloha. Happiness and warmth surged through the crowd. To experience a Boat Day was like arriving for the first time. Even the memory lifts my heart. I can hear the brisk brasses of the band in the merry rhythms of a hula as the ship eased in. Her rows of passengers laughed and waved as the lines were thrown and she slowed to rest. When the space between ship and shore was almost closed, the sounds and excitement heightened in a clamor of recognition, joyful tears and calling of names as searchers found each other. Flowers were thrown and confetti clouds burst open. Paper serpentine sprayed out from the ship to be caught by folk on the dock. The thin streamers looked like frail but loving strands, tenderly drawing the liner to land. And when the band finally played "Aloha Oe," many a burly man wiped a tear from his eye.

Once I watched a pretty island girl struggle out of the crush on the gangway to throw herself into her father's waiting arms. She was sobbing with her joy and the man held her, overwhelmed by the emotion. His hard old hands stroked her hair and when at last he spoke his voice chided huskily with love:

"Eh . . . whassamatta you, dear heart? I breeng you from far place to home, and now you cry . . . "

A shipfitter is one whose work is to lay out, fabricate, and put into position the structural parts of a ship, in readiness for riveting or welding them into place. He might be described more succinctly as a carpenter working in iron and steel.

I asked for a transfer to the shipfitters' shop and got it. I wanted to work with the big steel. It seemed somehow more important, permanent. Shipfitters fashioned the flesh and bone of warships, work that was basic to everything else.

I had often watched them cutting, shaping and hanging the heavy pieces; sculpting ponderous sheets and bars into hull-plates, frames, platforms and decking. I marveled at how the huge bulks were molded when white hot and how the burners' torches spit metal like a million jewels. I liked to watch chippers' hammers carving shiny bevels, and heavy wedges slammed down to force pieces of steel together. The work in sheet metal seemed like cutting paper dolls by comparison. A "tin knocker" needed scant protection from his thin and malleable material. But a shipfitter needed muscular riggers to shift his work a few feet, cranes to hoist it, and thick gloves, boots and goggles to keep it from maiming or even killing him. He required sledgehammers, huge shears and incredible heat to shape the immensities, and flatcars to carry them away. He feared and respected his material, dealt daily with implacable strengths, moved cautiously under monstrous weights.

A shipfitter started with large thick rectangles of metal, slabs without distinction. He studied his blueprint, measured distances on surfaces with great care, then marked his decisions on the steel with punch pricks or chalk lines. Blocks and tackle then moved the pieces to massive shears that made their cuts with earth-shaking smashes. Or the sheets were given to burners for more intricate shapings. And these acts were irrevocable, utterly final.

Big steel was forced, slowly and painfully, into the forms desired, and it resisted, fought every fraction of the way, was ever ready to crush, gash, blister or burn. Big steel was always a battle. But at the end, a reward was waiting, intimate and special.

It came when your gun platform, new decking or hull plate was wheeled from the shop to the drydock or pierside. Whistles blew and bystanders scattered when the crane lifted the threatening mass high. Riggers shouted and signaled, lines hummed with strain, and you urged, coaxed, cursed and prayed the awkward, inert thing into position—and the reward came when you saw it settle, fitting snugly, new and strong, *belonging*, and knew your work had been done well. In some strange way it was a victory. Always, there was extraordinary, almost mystical meaning in your casual command to the welder to make first attachment: "O.K. Tack it."

And the welder would nod, squinting as he bent to the task, flipping his mask down over his face. Light danced eerily on his Martian's head as he secured your work, making it one with the living ship.

ADMIRAL ISOROKU YAMAMOTO was named Commander in Chief of the Japanese Fleet in mid-August of 1939, two weeks before Hitler's armies marched into Poland.

He graduated from Itajima Naval College in 1904 when he was twenty. In 1928 he was assigned to the aircraft carrier *Akagi* and diligently studied aviation tactics. Later he attended Harvard University, then served at the Japanese embassy in Washington. He became a rear admiral at the age of forty-four.

Yamamoto was appointed vice-minister of the Imperial Navy in 1937. In this position he was threatened with assassination because of what his critics interpreted as antiwar statements. In cold fact, he was advocating caution and preparedness because he deeply respected the power and ingenuity of America. More than once he said publicly that conflict with the United States or Great Britain at that time could lead only to disaster for Japan. Japanese extremists accused him of being pro-American.

But during his service as vice-minister, then as fleet commander, the expansion and modernization of Japan's navy went forward rapidly. Two large aircraft carriers were being built and long-range bombing planes were placed in service. The Zero fighter was developed under tightest security. Huge modern battleships were being constructed—almost twice the size of existing Japanese ships. But Yamamoto compared these dreadnoughts to ancient religious scrolls hung in homes: "Of no proven worth," he said. "A matter of faith ... of as much use in modern warfare as the sword of a samurai. . . . "

Yamamoto was the most outspoken advocate of aircraft in a shoal of battleship admirals. He was a man of the present, not bound by old ways. Among many imaginative steps he took was expansion of Japan's "tactical" defense line to more than a thousand miles east of the Marshall Islands, to include Hawaii. Also, he was successful in combining all elements of the Japanese fleet into one unified command. In 1941 that command was his, and the depth of respect in which he was held by his men and his peers was immense.

Yamamoto had a reputation as a remarkably successful poker player. And once, surreptitiously, he had the chairs of junior officers sprinkled with thumb tacks, to illustrate the effectiveness of surprise.

On a day in January of 1941, Admiral Yamamoto sat quietly in his quarters on the battleship *Nagato*.

Above his desk was pinned a map of the Hawaiian archipelago. At his hand was a considerable amount of up-to-date information about America's Pacific Fleet: the movements of its ships and air patrols, the schedules governing ship and shore life, the details of training programs, facts of geography and data about weather—all the minutiae of routines of the 14th Naval District of the United States in Hawaii.

Undoubtedly, Yamamoto thought deeply. Quite likely he pondered much about the pressures that certain countries of the Western world were forcing on his intensely patriotic and ambitious homeland. Surely, he probed deep into his private dilemmas, his personal convictions, his awareness of duty to the emperor and Japan. All his days of striving, his years of training, his lifetime of commitment—and the course of a larger history—were pushing him now to make an extraordinary decision.

He rubbed an ink stick on a wetted stone and picked up a brush.

Then, in three pages of neat calligraphy, he wrote a plan for a surprise attack upon the United States Fleet at Pearl Harbor.

Admiral Takejiro Onishi, air chief of the Imperial Navy, studied his commander's startling proposal. Admiral Yamamoto's instructions to him had been brief: "Make it work."

Onishi knew exactly the man best qualified for such an assignment. He summoned Commander Minoru Genda, air officer of the carrier *Akagi.*

Genda was in his thirties, his brilliance as a tactician unquestioned, his dedication complete. Photos of the time show him to have been a handsome man, slim and fine-featured, with penetrating dark eyes. Flying was his whole life. The plan pleased and excited him.

His thinking had been moving in much the same direction for a long time. The British air assault on the Italian Navy at Taranto in November of 1940 had impressed him enormously. In less than an hour, twenty-three small planes from the carrier *Illustrious* had torpedoed three Italian battleships, two cruisers, and their auxiliary vessels, severely reducing Mussolini's sea power.

Genda went immediately and enthusiastically to work.

Less than two weeks later he returned his assessment of the problem, with supporting ideas, to Admiral Onishi. He said the Pearl Harbor plan would be difficult to carry out, but not impossible.

Genda stressed to Onishi that the element of surprise was paramount and that an attack on Pearl Harbor would be most effective at dawn.

All available aircraft carriers should be employed and a dive-bomber attack on the ships at anchor would be most destructive. High-level bombers and fighter protection would also be needed, but dive bombers had priority. Torpedo bombers were a very attractive possibility, he suggested. But there were obstacles: A torpedo plane's approach to the ships anchored along Ford Island would have to be an extremely short and low-level run. Presumably, the Americans would have torpedo net protection. And Pearl Harbor itself was shallow. Torpedos then in use would more likely plunge into the harbor's bottom than hit the target ships.

Above all else he emphasized the need for absolute secrecy in preparing and sailing a mammoth task force over thousands of miles of ocean to strike at the very heart of an enemy. The gamble was monumental. Failure could mean the loss of precious units of Japan's navy. Failure would leave the way clear for massive retaliatory strikes. Failure might even mean catastrophe for cities and people of the Japanese homeland.

With in a small and select group, Admiral Yamamoto's plan was dissected, discussed and debated.

Meanwhile, a move most annoying to anti-air admirals was the separation from their forces and control of five aircraft carriers and ten escort destroyers. These were then designated as the First Air Fleet.

None of the old line-officers knew anything about "Operation Hawaii." Even Vice-Admiral Chuichi Nagumo, chosen to head the new air fleet, was amazed when informed of the plan and held strong reservations about its possibilities for success. He did not believe that a huge task force could be sailed undetected across thousands of miles of the Pacific Ocean. He hoped that diplomatic negotiations in progress with the United States would solve Japan's problems. And he felt certain that Yamamoto's daring scheme would be blocked by their superiors on the General Staff.

Conditions worsened for the Empire. Japan's armies in northern Indochina had moved to take over that whole country. President Roosevelt's retaliation was to freeze all Japanese assets in the United States and forbid the sale of oil to Japan. These acts, along with previous embargoes on iron and other scrap metals, were soon throttling the Empire. With only one year's supply of oil on hand, her military power and industrial plants faced strangulation. The United States refused to lift the embargo unless Japan withdrew from Indochina and China itself, where the war with Chiang Kai-shek's armies was in its fourth year. To the Japanese, American demands were unacceptable, not only economically, but as a threat to national honor. Even listening to them was insulting, a loss of face.

In August of 1940, a team of U.S. cryptologists, operating under the cover name of MAGIC, had achieved the near-impossible: They produced the complete translation of a message sent in an extremely complicated machine-cipher used by the Japanese. The Americans had, in effect, broken the Japanese diplomatic code.

Distribution of the MAGIC translations was restricted to President Roosevelt and a small circle of his high-level advisors. By 1941, only a few of the incredibly complex machines needed to decode the messages had been finished. The ability to decode the interceptions gave the United States enormous advantages over the Japanese.

But there were drawbacks too. For one, Washington authorities considered the intercepts as diplomatic communications, without military import, mainly useful in dictating American political response. For another, all too often intercepts received at in-between stations were relayed to Washington by ordinary air mail. Furthermore, the time needed for translations into English sometimes led to long delays. One intercept took as many as fifty-nine days to process.

Perhaps the greatest drawback of all was the fact that Admiral Husband E. Kimmel and General Walter C. Short, commanders of the naval and army forces in Hawaii, were not on the list of recipients for MAGIC's intelligence. They did not even know that the operation existed.

To his people, Emperor Hirohito was a deity, a direct descendant of the Japanese sun goddess. It is difficult for westerners to understand the awe induced in his subjects by his simple presence. It cowed dignitaries of the highest rank, imbued any gathering with an aura of holiness.

In early September of 1941 the Emperor sat on a dais above a meeting of his civilian and military advisers. He did not move, nor did he speak.

In a previous meeting, the prime minister, Prince Konoye, had informed his imperial majesty that the United States would not agree to a summit meeting unless satisfactory preliminary agreements had been settled between the two governments. American stipulations were all heavily in favor of American wishes. Still, Konoye hoped that the emperor would persuade the military men to abandon plans for further encroachment in the South Pacific while negotiations continued. At this time, the emperor had not been informed about Admiral Yamamoto's plan for an attack on Pearl Harbor.

During his conference with Konoye, Hirohito had been obviously troubled. He was astonished, he said, that plans for war were superseding diplomatic explorations to solve differences.

But now, in this meeting of the Imperial Staff, the emperor's "divine radiance" prohibited his speaking. The words he wanted to say were uttered for him by a subordinate. Hirohito sat, stiffly, seemingly impassive, thick spectacles glistening over his black moustache. He listened while Konoye read a paper titled "A Plan For National Policy."

When Konoye finished, Baron Hara, speaking for the emperor, said the throne had the impression that hopes of peace appeared to have been abandoned—that the emphasis was now upon war rather than diplomatic negotiations.

The Minister of the Navy assured his emperor that this was not the case. But two of the other top military commanders present remained adamantly silent.

Then an act of stunning significance occurred. The emperor rose to speak. The gathering was astounded, galvanized into a shocked silence.

The emperor said he regretted that the high command had not seen fit to make the situation clear. He drew a small piece of paper from his pocket and told the assembly it was part of a poem written by his grandfather, the Emperor Meiji. In his slow, high-pitched official voice, he read:
"Since we are all brothers in the world,
Why are the winds and waves so unsettled?"

Later, Konoye wrote that the meeting ended in an atmosphere of "unprecedented tenseness."

The annual war games at the Naval College were advanced several months to mid-September. Ten admirals, seven captains, and almost two dozen commanders assembled for the exercises. Only a few knew that the Yamamoto-Genda plan for the attack upon Pearl Harbor would be discussed.

The surprise-attack proposal was received with mild interest and little enthusiasm. None of the top officers outside Admiral Yamamoto's air-minded faction displayed either favor or optimism, but they agreed to include the problem in the games.

Three approach routes suggested by Genda were assessed. The first was a southern approach, through the Marshall Islands; the second, a central route passing Midway Island; the third, northern toward the Aleutians, then down south past Midway.

Admiral Nagumo voiced preference for the southern route, remarking that unpredictable winter weather in the north would militate against success. Genda politely pointed out that this was exactly what American admirals might be thinking. Nagumo agreed to try the Aleutian approach for the first game.

The initial run-through, using model ships on charts, showed the attack to be a failure. The "U.S. team" discovered the task force in the morning and fighters shot down half the Japanese aircraft. Two carriers were sunk and other ships took heavy damage.

But a second simulated run, using the same approach on a painfully precise schedule, gave the Japanese fleet night cover when it came within reach of American aircraft in Hawaii. Complete surprise was attained. The umpire ruled that U.S. losses were heavy and that Japan's forces escaped without harm.

On October 17th, 1941, General Hideki Tojo replaced a weak and wavering Prince Konoye as prime minister. The general's pugnacious militarism evidenced itself almost immediately. Japanese complaints and demands were repeated and intensified: America was choking off her supplies of vital materials; America must acknowledge Japan's leadership in Asia, withdraw support of Chiang Kai-shek, and recognize Japan's presence in Manchuria. The Tojo government accused the United States of "unpardonable crimes" against the Empire. Other outraged voices said Japan would be reduced to the ignominy of a fourth-rate power. Joseph Grew, the U.S. Ambassador in Tokyo, cabled a warning to Washington that Japan might adopt dramatic and dangerous measures, would even risk national suicide rather than lose face to America.

Japan's ambassador in Washington was a well-intentioned retired admiral, Kichisaburo Nomura. He was without diplomatic training and had been posted by Prince Konoye simply because he had made many American friends, including Franklin Roosevelt, during his naval career. The elderly Nomura was becoming overwhelmed with the mounting stresses of his office. A MAGIC intercept revealed to Americans that he found it difficult to live under the pressures and wished to be relieved. Tojo kept him on, but did appoint a veteran diplomat, Saburo Kurusu, to assist in Washington negotiations. Kurusu was the man who had earlier signed the Tripartite Agreement in Berlin, binding Japan to Nazi Germany and Fascist Italy.

Among Admiral Yamamoto's colleagues many still opposed the Pearl Harbor plan. Wars at sea were fought with battleships, they insisted. Wars at sea had always been fought with battleships. Sailors had brine in their blood, not air . . .

Their doubts were expressed. Angry winter weather in the north Pacific would make refueling a task force impossible. It was too late for such an attack. Diplomatic talks with America were breaking down and surely the enemy's fleet was on the alert.

The risks were immense; far better to concentrate on acquiring the precious oil and metal riches of the Dutch East Indies with minimal opposition. The arguments were many and varied: the glowering Soviets threatened; aircraft carriers were too thinly armored; conceivably, the Americans were luring Japan into a trap...

In October, Yamamoto sent a letter to his superiors on the General Staff, all of whom were opposed to the plan. He wrote:
"The presence of the U.S. Fleet in Hawaii is a dagger pointed at our throats .... The Hawaii operation is absolutely indispensable .... "

When the hedging and objections continued, he took his boldest step. He dispatched a senior staff-officer to his chiefs with the demand that a decision be made. Time was running out, he said. He must have an answer immediately. When the old arguments were recited anew, Yamamoto's advocate played his ace on November 3rd. He said that his admiral insisted that the plan be adopted. If it was not accepted, Yamamoto would refuse to be held responsible for the consequences of the rejection; he would resign and take his entire staff with him.

The threat staggered the decision makers. The need for an answer spiraled up to one man, Chief-of-Staff Nagano. The prospect of losing Yamamoto was unthinkable, inconceivable. He answered "Yes."

In Japan, a training area near the southern port-city of Kagoshima was selected.

An island in its bay served to represent Ford Island in Pearl Harbor. Other topographic features in the area were similar to those at Pearl. A department store in Kagoshima simulated taller structures near Pearl Harbor's repair basin.

Over and over again, every day, bombers screamed down over mountains similar to Oahu's Koolaus, skimming treetops and dropping dummy bombs in the water. Householders in the area complained that the continuous roars of aircraft were dismantling their frail homes. Farmers grumbled that chickens had stopped laying eggs. Geisha girls, their tatami mats trembling, were torn between charms of the handsome young pilots and a not entirely unjustified concern for the shattering of their fragile tea-houses.

At the same time, in other locations, high-level bombers were practicing; and dive bombers, time after time, plunged into almost vertical drops, until they were able to discharge loads and pull out at the unheard-of height of 1,500 feet.

To Minoru Genda fell the responsibility of choosing a man to lead the attack force. He would have liked to take the command for himself, but his position as staff officer prohibited that. He selected one of his classmates, twenty-nine-year-old Commander Mitsuo Fuchida. Fuchida had an impeccable record, with valuable experience in the China war and more than 3,000 hours of air-time. Genda's choice was excellent, for in addition to his experience, Fuchida was a born leader. He inspired unquestioning confidence and was loved by his airmen. They would follow him anywhere, do anything he ordered.

As time eased by at Pearl we came to know all the ships that homed to its lochs: the coal-burning tender *Ontario;* the four-stack destroyers *Zane,*

Wasmuth, Perry, Conyngham and *Trever;* the
"birdboat" minesweepers, *Swan, Widgeon,*
Bobolink and *Tern;* repair ships like the *Vestal,*
Kukui, Rigel and *Dobbin;* aging cruisers, *Raleigh,*
Richmond, Detroit, and the great gray battleships
Maryland, Oklahoma, Arizona, Tennessee,
Nevada and *West Virginia.*

Our tasks took from a few hours to many
weeks, depending on the needs of the ships. Jobs
varied from hull repair to installing new decking,
gun mounts and ammunition stowage. Most of
the ships were quite old and all the battleships were
of World War I vintage. The *Nevada,* for example,
had been launched in 1914, the *Vestal* in 1908
and the *Utah* a year later. The minelayer *Oglala*
had been built in 1907 and had served the historic
Fall River Line as the *Massachusetts.* Sometimes
our chores were done in the open, but most of these
elderly vessels needed surgery in their innards,
where work conditions were the worst. Labor on
these oldtimers often meant prickly sweat,
stinging sparks and stifling hours in dark bottoms
and grease-lined tanks. And burns, cuts and aches,
and bouts of vomiting from smoke poisons. But,
in glancing back, the painful experiences are not
among the sharpest memories. Clearest of all are
the better times—days bright and right, full of
banter over potent coffee in smudged mugs,
discovery of Hawaii and ourselves, laughter
with friends . . .

On night shifts we took supper breaks at
the Yard Cafeteria. Dim figures straggled up
unlighted roads from the shops and ships. Behind
us the fleet settled down to sleep. Ships along
Battleship Row were like phantoms, pinpoints of

The Shirley Temple-Metro
deal is hot again and the studio
is cooking up a Rooney-
Garland-Temple story, another
of those kid musicals . . . .

1

Eleanor Roosevelt Hopes To Visit Hawaii

Irvingston, N.J. (UP)—The body of William Weismann, at 44 one of the last of the Prohibition Era's mobsters, was found Saturday night wrapped in a bloody sheet on the floor of an expensive sedan . . . .

"It has often been said that the Island of Oahu is so thoroughly ringed with defenses it would be impossible for hostile planes to come over the Islands. Their approach would be detected long before they were in striking distance, and if they ever got over the city the Army and Navy would make quick work of them before they returned to their bases, presumably ships at sea . . . . In these days of tense expectancy, the presence of Uncle Sam's Army and Navy in powerful array, brings to civilians a restful sense of security . . . . "

—*Paradise of the Pacific*
Honolulu, May, 1941

3

TOTAL
OF 187 OAHU
DRAFTEES
ARE
INDUCTED

4

5

MANY PERSONS
IN HAWAII AFFECTED
AS U.S.
FREEZES
JAPANESE ASSETS

Three Douglas DC3 24-passenger land planes flew from Oakland for use here by Hawaiian Airlines between the Islands. The flight was 13 hours, 53 minutes, representing a new Pacific record . . . . It also represented the longest overwater delivery of land planes . . . .

Mary Astor Steals
Film From Bette Davis

Pearl Harbor
Highway
To Be
Safest In Territory
Six Lanes
Planned

6

Advice To Aliens In Hawaii (an editorial):

Aliens in Honolulu and throughout Hawaii are being told they need not fear any form of abuse if this country should go to war, particularly with Japan. . . . We do not believe they have any cause for alarm now or in the future . . . .

7

Aldrich Family
Begins
Fourth Season
On Air

EDITOR, THE HONOLULU ADVERTISER:

" . . . as far as I know from nine years in the Japanese language school I have never heard one of my teachers speak of loyalty to Japan (in fact we have been taught to respect the American Flag, our democracy and our privileges). The language school I attend has taught me to be respectable and honest in whatever we undertake.

Please don't call us New Americans, friends, because we are just as American as you are.

From my very soul,
Charlotte Kimie"

"TEN YEARS AGO AN AIRPLANE FLIGHT
from San Francisco or Los Angeles to
Honolulu was considered hazardous. Today
it is routine. Not only do the commercial
clippers ferry back and forth on time, except
in stormy weather, but Navy planes do the
hop in sixes and twelves, flying in formation
all the way . . . . The American continent
has moved appreciably closer to our
archipelago through almost daily passenger
and mail service . . . . Who knows but that
within a few years you will board your clipper
in Honolulu for New York City non-stop?"
—*Paradise of the Pacific*, September, 1941

8

Sergeant York Proposes
Jail For Lindbergh

Jamestown, Tenn., Sept 13 (UP)—Alvin
York, the lanky Tennessee World War he-
ro, said tonight that Charles E. Lindbergh
and Sen. Gerald Nye, Rep., N.D., "ought
to be shut up by throwing them square into jail—today and not tomorrow . . . . "

9

TED WILLIAMS CLOSES SEASON WITH .406 MARK

FLEET CHIEF SAYS HAWAII FAILING JOB
Kimmel Charges Islands Malinger As Nation Threatened... in a forthright talk to members of the Honolulu Chamber of Commerce and their guests at the Royal Hawaiian Hotel ... Admiral Kimmel, pulling no punches, declared that Hawaii has led a soft life and hopes to continue that life, unwilling to face the realities of a world at war ....

10

Louis
Stops Nova
In Sixth
To
Defend
Title

Robert Sherwood
has completely
rewritten "There
Shall Be No
Night," and the
Lunts will
probably take
it on tour
again . . . .

11   12

The deportation
of Harry Bridges,
West Coast
CIO leader, on
grounds of
membership in
the Communist
Party, has been
recommended . . . .

13

light limning their outlines. Other craft at rest in the repair basin were quiet, naked bulbs glowing like haloes over a few listless sailors on gang-watch duty.

But the cafeteria bloomed with light and sound. The food was cursed ritually, and the proprietor provoked to a fit of outrage with our insults. The juke box blared Roy Acuff songs, Benny Goodman hits and "San Antonio Rose." The two ripe Portuguese counter-girls flagrantly added extra beef to the gravy-like stew of favorite clients. There was endless skirmishing between lovers of hillbilly music and swing-band fans. And inevitable talk about the girls in the new crop of tourists, or the exoticity of island-grown mixtures of Orientals, Whites and Hawaiians.

We came to better know our locally-born fellow workers too. Many had migrated to Honolulu from neighbor islands, and they told us about the plantation towns and how people lived in the tiny communities that had grown up around sugar mills and company stores. In these talks we "mainlanders" got our first inkling of the great spaces still to be found in Hawaii, the pattern of their days and fabrics of life for small groups of people amid the vastness of sugar and pineapple fields.

Instinctively, we sat together, all of us who were young, away from home for the first time and sensed that Pearl Harbor was a stage in our lives. Surely, we knew what was going on in a larger world. But young people owned a larger naiveté in those days before instant communications came along to make even children so wise. Distant cataclysms entered more gently into our

consciousness, their full meanings were never
clear. There were no nightly films in color about
Jews being beaten or rounded up for concentration
camps, no newscasts about a Nazi ring of steel
strangling Leningrad. There was radio talk about
a possible meeting between President Roosevelt
and Japan's prime minister, Konoye, to "settle
differences"—and surely American nervousness
in the Pacific was reflected in the nature of our
work at Pearl. Hawaii's newspapers almost daily
featured stories about states-of-emergency and
martial law in the event of trouble. But, we thought
and argued, these threats certainly could not be
serious. Surely, the Men In Charge had everything
under control. Meanwhile, there were fresh
recordings to enjoy by the Dorseys, Sinatra, Louis
Armstrong and the Andrews Sisters. Ted Williams
was hitting .400 and promoter Mike Jacobs was
predicting a million-dollar gate for the Joe Louis-
Lou Nova fight. We were learning to ride the surf
at Waikiki and play ukuleles while we flirted
with dark-eyed wahines on brown-sugar sand.
Gone With The Wind was playing at the Waikiki
Theater and we saw the spectacle of Atlanta
burning and marveled at the wonders Hollywood
could perform.

One or two mornings a week the giant
Pan American Clipper lumbered over the calm of
Middle Loch, churning up a wide wake, then
climbing to hang high over the Molokai Channel
off Diamond Head. The flying boat appeared to
be motionless in the sky although she was moving
at a fantastic 175 miles per hour.

What a wonder that was! Only eighteen
hours to California!

Noland and I had rented a room from a scatter-brained divorcee in a house a few doors off the beach on Kealohilani Avenue. She was a blowzy sort and we called her The Widow. Apparently she lived on erratic alimony payments between haphazard outings as a saleslady, so she was happy to have the added income we brought. The Widow's interests were gin and phonograph records, in that order. Bing Crosby's versions of "Sweet Leilani" and "Blue Hawaii" were big hits at the time and she played them constantly. Being in her late thirties, she seemed almost elderly to us and we spent little more than sleeping time in her untidy bungalow.

The Waikiki Tavern was our social center. Incongruously Alpine in design, the peaked and timbered structure sat at the water's edge, a salted stucco, a bit warped by spray. A dining room opened out on the ocean side and a bar decorated with couplets from the *Rubaiyat* bordered the street. Next door were the rooms of the Waikiki Inn, largely a hot-bed operation in three or four stories. Under the Inn was an odorous basement where lockers, surfboards and bathing suits were rented and shrimp-size scorpions abounded. The Inn's rentals were made mostly to tourists on the cheap or husbands on a frolic.

But the Tavern was *the* neighborhood bar. Its patrons felt quite at home and it had the added attraction of being the only decent saloon within blocks. The surroundings were comfortable and worn, with a shoes-off feeling, and the clientele ran the range of people who drink. The fearsome, Neanderthal countenance of Harry D., the bouncer, served to keep order. In reality, Harry was as

violent as a mouse. Any day, one could find beachboys and their current inamoratas, a parched
tourist or two, action seekers from Honolulu's
more sheltered neighborhoods, and local folks from
Waikiki's sidestreets. Other faithful customers
were the few servicemen and their wives who lived
near the beach. The Tavern opened in late morning
and stayed busy until midnight, later on weekends.
One could always find a friend or a happening
at the Tavern.

The nearby Moana Hotel was a far more
dignified establishment, large, white, and vaguely
colonial, with a columned porte-cochère over a
crescent front drive. On the beach side a courtyard
embraced by wide verandas surrounded a big
banyan tree. Here, you could laze and drink beer
in shade while studying the surfers out to sea
or girls closer to hand. The Moana was a fine
spot for establishing liaisons, an acceptable staging
area where meetings were easy and natural.
Occasionally we would don jackets and go there for
dinner. The spacious dining room was airy and
genteel, part of it extending over the sand.
Oriental waiters wore black ties and silver service
gleamed on glossy linen. Those evenings gave us a
feeling of being very worldly and sophisticated.

On other nights we trudged farther down
the beach, to sit on the seawall and listen to Harry
Owens's orchestra at the Royal Hawaiian. On one
side of us lay the deserted ocean. On the other
were beautifully-gowned women, white-jacketed
escorts, glistening crystal, and popping corks—all
in a setting of expensive ease. The Royal
represented everything that was rich, desirable
and luxurious—all the things that we too, would

have some day. But at the time it was too much
of an extravagance for us, strictly the province
of wealthy visitors and those who were at home
in Honolulu's citadels of commerce.

Our days lost their names.

They became gentle spaces in which the
sun rose, traveled and then departed, moving its
brilliance to farther islands. Palm trunks turned
powder blue in twilight. Horizon clouds underwent
delicate changes from golds to greens and purples.

As night came, a few neon signs sputtered
to life along Kalakaua Avenue. Lacy light from
streetlamps filtered through crowns of trees. The
soft glows from shops and cottages bathed
passing strollers. Late swimmers and surfers,
expelled by dark from the ocean, padded home
on bare feet. The cooings of tiny barred doves
were like love moans as the dainty birds settled to
rest. Mynahs gossiped briefly, a hidden rabble in
the balloons of banyans. Along the Kuhio seawall,
the old card players dealt fresh hands, ignoring
the hour. The first bursts of revelry bounced from
the Waikiki Tavern and traffic on the avenue
thinned to a few tardy homegoers. Sidestreet
houses emitted little eruptions of children's play,
ukulele plunkings, radio music and kitchen
sounds that promised supper.

Footloose and financially flush after our
unaccustomed paydays, we tried to swallow the
evening town. Our usual start was a ride into
Honolulu to the Alexander Young Hotel Roof
Garden. A cheerful chap named Giggie Royse led
its orchestra and featured a singer named Napua

Stevens. Napua seemed the loveliness of all
island girls in one, a ripe-mango beauty with raven
hair and skin like tinted ivory. The warm and
expansive Giggie took frequent breaks for revival
at the bar where he chatted and joked with us.
But Napua was unapproachable, either
chaperoned by protective parents or in the
custody of a stalwart fiancé from the
police force.

Haoles dominated the Young's clientele.
There was a fair number of others with Hawaiian
blood, and a few, very few, Orientals. In one
way or another, most of the youthful crowd had
some kind of family involvement in the cross-
fertilized plantation and merchant interests
controlling Hawaii. Almost all had attended private
Punahou School or Caucasian-flavored Roosevelt
High, and theirs was a closed society, courteous
but aloof. There were cracks in its walls for
personable young military officers and other
newcomers properly introduced, but no openings
for brash young interlopers without visible
credentials, like ourselves. So we would sit there,
hating the confident young ensigns and lieutenants
in all their gold-barred glory, taking our solace in
Giggie's music and Napua's tender vocalizing.
Always frustrated, we would soon leave, to seek
warmer welcomes elsewhere.

These were easily found at The Black Cat,
Hoffman's, Bill Lederer's, The Pantheon, Mint,
and other taverns in the Hotel Street environs.
So we visited one or several, and drank, debated,
lied and laughed the hours away. Invariably we
ran into navy friends or fellow-workers from Pearl.
And when the bars closed we took the exile in

swaggering stride. Iron-bellied and indestructible, we refused to let the day escape.

Honolulu went to bed early then, becoming a near-deserted city. Most of its inhabitants withdrew to back rooms or upper floors; others returned to hillside and valley homes. A few cinemas stayed open, and Chinatown spluttered into life for a few hours. But after ten o'clock activity was on the wane almost everywhere. By eleven, most cafes closed, poolrooms were shuttering up and the last few enthusiastic holdouts were being jollied out of the cathouses. Even the bars called time at midnight.

But when the saloons darkened and other latches clicked, many smaller stirrings of life remained, and we walked among them: spills of light, muffled mumbles of a dice game and complaint of an imprisoned fighting-cock. In its latest hours the tropic city remained alive with tickles of music, mothers' murmurs, children's coughs and the giggling of lovers. And we prowled streets aimlessly, searching ultramarine hours, crossing ponds of light under streetlamps, walking without threat or danger where the only sounds were our footsteps. Our talk rambled as much as we did, and we mused the age-old wonderings of young men: who we were and what made us, and where we were going and what we would someday do. We talked of childhoods and first loves and families, of times past and times to come; of conquests, needs, discoveries; and of Wendell Willkie, FDR, Father Coughlin and Hitler. We agreed and disagreed, scattering our wondrously naive opinions about like gravel. Comfortably different, from different places and makings, we fed thoughts and jokes and bits of learning to each other. And sometimes we only sang tipsy songs at the Hawaiian moon.

Once, at the end of such a night, when a chill moved down from the hills and a soft rain brushed the city, we took refuge in one of the little all-night saimin stands, and sat at bare-board tables among the sullen, distant night-people, lifting the hot noodles high on chopsticks and drinking the briny broth. I remember how we looked at one another and began to laugh. People around us stopped eating and stared. We laughed on, not knowing why, laughing about everything and nothing, about nothing at all.

PART TWO

FLOWERINGS

"Now, today, in this good year of 1941, in the midst of troublous times and dire threat of war, a new element of activity has come into the community... almost beyond belief of the kamaaina (oldtime) citizen.... It is a fair average if he recognizes ten faces in the parade .... The tempo of business has been accelerated. People walk faster along the streets, traffic problems should develop with the influx of cars. Yes, it is different. What started at Waikiki a hundred or more years ago has spread all over the Honolulu area. Time, constant advertising, thousands of visitors over the years and finally, a National Defense Program, have transformed Honolulu from a small town to a bustling city."

—*Paradise of the Pacific*, July, 1941

A time came when our salty chauffeur, Captain Ernie, sold his car and disappeared.

The Oahu Railway, originally a pineapple hauler, began running trains for Pearl Harbor commuters, and we soon dubbed it the Toonerville Trolley. The sky would still be dark as the cars grumbled out of Iwilei in the sleeping city. The train was like a toy, clattering over narrow tracks, its whistle stabbing the morning. Passengers were only fuzzy shapes, stumbling for seats or gathering in twos and threes on platforms. Cigarets glowed and iron wheels clicked as we sped out over the marshes inland from Keehi Lagoon.

By then, hints of dawn would be pinking the sky. Soft light outlined the mountains and small sampans were photo-still on dark shallows. Companions were recognized and conversation brightened. Marines and sailors who had spent the night in Honolulu would be lethargic from hangovers or rehashing their adventures. Most were single men, shacking up with local girlfriends or sacking-in at the River Street whorehouses. The doxies often took on overnight tricks at a special rate, or merely to banish the bordello blues.

And the servicemen talked:

"Fifty screws a day and she told me she gets *lonesome!*"

". . . a Carolina girl, for Chrissake, from right near home."

Just past Hickam Field the train stopped and marines from Pearl swung aboard. With 45s sagging at their hips they walked the aisles, examining faces and badge photos. Then the train jerked on into the shipyard and passengers peeled off at shops or duty stations along the way.

The main gate no longer looked as it had when we arrived almost a year before. New buildings were popping up almost weekly. A big new cantonment, called "Boys Town," had been raised nearby to house the swell of workers. Most of the Boys Town men were older than our Waikiki crowd. Their lives revolved around jobs and bosses, nights in the barracks, meals in messhalls, and beer, booze and dice for diversion. Occasionally they might spend an evening on the town or take a dip in the ocean. But most of the new arrivals were in Hawaii only for the money they could make and rarely left the area. I heard it said more than once that the crap game at Boys Town went on for years, day and night, without interruption.

Competition for the best looking wahines in Waikiki was intense. But my roommate, Noland, was a handsome chap with a disarmingly shy smile. Within months he had charmed his way into romance with a slim Korean girl. Pearl-toothed and with milk-chocolate skin, she was almost always in a bathing suit, displaying her seductive best. I envied him. I did poorly with girls, too eager, perhaps, awkward and crass in my Boston-Irish stiffness. I managed a few brief tumbles with tipsy tourists and other transient tarts, but these were considerably less than soul-soaring experiences.

Generally, prizes on the beach gravitated to suave and worldly Casanovas, those cursed young army and navy officers, or the Hawaiian beachboys. The beachboys triumphed most often. Their don't-give-a-damn attitude, guitar-strumming and expertise with song, surfboard, and lomilomi massage made them irresistible. Splendid physiques didn't damage their chances either. They formed a tight group, of which the famous Olympic swimming champion, Duke Kahanamoku was paterfamilias. This sandstrip aristocracy held only about a dozen members and their exclusiveness was legend. They were dedicated hedonists, expansive and garrulous, big and friendly. Nevertheless, they would cheerfully break the leg of any freelancer who dared invade their monopoly on surfing lessons and other aquatic hustles.

Finding girls was only one of our problems. For a long time we newcomers were a social curiosity too.

We were haoles, yes, but very different from haole tourists except for our aura of impermanence. We certainly did not belong to the oldtimer, kamaaina-class haoles who had lived in the islands for generations. Nor could we be conveniently tucked among the Orientals, Filipinos, or Portuguese who had been indentured over decades to cut the cane and pluck the pineapples. Also, we were separated by language, with our smattering of slangs, twangs and drawls. Island pidgin was in common use, an exotic kind of basic English overlaid with Hawaiian and salted with contributions from other mother-tongues. "Eh, Bool!" a worker would shout, "Poot da-kine eenside da puka!" meaning, "Hey, Bull! Put that in the hole!"

Localites found our regional accents just as amusing and confusing.

"Chee! You guys talk funny-kine Eenglish" a Chinese would say to an Alabama man—and there would be laughter all around, bringing us together. In time most of us learned bits and pieces of pidgin and practiced it to more laughter. And eventually we acquired a label of our own, clearly needed for a human slab afloat in island society. "Defense Workers," we were called. No one could think of a better name.

But even after nearly a year on the scene many island girls continued to shy away from us. Mostly this came from circumspection about all haoles, particularly newcomers. The establishment haoles were the owners, supervisors and social arbiters, and had been within the memory of almost everyone. Conversely, almost all transient whites of the past century had been aggressively horny and/or drunken whalers, traders, beach-combers, Bible salesmen, or other wastrels with wicked designs. Island mothers had been warning daughters about that kind of haole for more than a hundred years. There was little reason to assume that young defense workers would be any different. Hawaiians were the warmest, most hospitable of all islanders—a virtue that had made them an endangered species—but most island Orientals remained withdrawn in a pride of religion

and culture. The petite waitresses and shopgirls
who smiled coyly and joked with us during the
day went home nightly to the domination of
parents raised in social ghettos during decades of
mannered caution. In 1941 there was still a
pervasive awareness of race and place even among
second- and third-generation offspring of immi-
grants. And the great majority of white men did
not work with their hands. Therefore, being our
kind of haole meant being suspect in the mass.
Many of Honolulu's neighborhoods had become
racial quiltings, their occupants living harmoni-
ously side by side. But Madeiran Portuguese
was still being spoken on the slopes of Punchbowl
and fluent Hawaiian was the language of lanes
in Papakolea and Kakaako. Japanese Buddhists
thronged their temples weekly, and many men
chattered voluble Cantonese over mahjong tiles
around Maunakea Street. These were pockets
where the old ways clung, islets of passive defiance
in a time of change.

In Hawaii's ports and towns and cashiers'
cages the changes were being felt in the nourish-
ment of new jobs, more money and added people.
Even so, the Territory of Hawaii was merely
peering over the fences of the twentieth century.
The major controls remained firmly in the hands
of descendants of the pioneer missionary and
trading families. The voices of power still spoke in
New England accents and the merchant aristocracy
lived in upper Nuuanu Valley or on estates along
restricted beachfronts and haughty hillsides. Their
enclaves were paternal and feudal, maintained
by Japanese maids, Chinese cooks and Filipino
gardeners. Admirals and generals were inducted

into society by way of intimate luncheons, or dinners at the staid and creaky Pacific Club. Weekends were saved for polo in the park, reunions at the family beach house or visits to cousins in the country. Sons and daughters were schooled, after Punahou, in Eastern universities. There was disquieting talk about "commie" labor organizers creeping about in the canefields and on the docks. And, of course, no one knew what those "damned Japs" were up to.

Otherwise, all was well with the world.

NONE OF THE AIRMEN at Kagoshima had an inkling about the real reason for their practice. Commander Fuchida told them they were being trained to torpedo ships anchored in shallow water. Even though no training torpedos were available, he said they must go through the motions. His specific instructions surprised the pilots: they were to climb to nearly 7,000 feet, assemble, then drop to "attack" the bay at rooftop height. After releasing their imaginary torpedos they would zoom up and away.

Meanwhile, technicians elsewhere were working day and night to create a torpedo that could be launched into the shallow waters of Pearl Harbor and cross them to hit the battleship targets. A special fin was being devised, so that the missiles would not bury themselves in the harbor's bottom. The first of these new torpedos would not be ready until mid-November. But each day the planes at Kagoshima screamed down, then dipped, dropping dummies.

The pilots thought all this was rather foolish, a waste of time. But no one presumed to question the exercise. Fuchida was offhand, completely calm. A fellow-officer who shared the secret of the attack plan said he would have made a marvelous actor.

The cost was $600 per month for the most important part of the spy effort that fed intelligence from Hawaii to Japan in 1941.

That sum was paid to Takeo Yoshikawa, a twenty-eight year-old naval ensign, retired for medical reasons, then trained carefully in espionage. For four years he had studied English. Also he had immersed himself in the world's major publications about warships, concentrating upon ship recognition. In addition, he was somewhat of an expert on America's Pacific bases.

Yoshikawa was assigned to the Japanese Consulate General in Honolulu in late March, 1941, under the cover of "vice-consul, Tadashi Morimura." The consul-general, Nagao Kita, was also a recent arrival, assigned from a post in China because his superiors believed that he would be more aggressive in espionage than his aging predecessor

The sudden appearance of Morimura-Yoshikawa piqued the curiosity of the Honolulu staff. He was not listed on the roster of Japanese diplomats, and he certainly did not behave like one. He was under thirty years of age, a drinker and a playboy who apparently took little if anything seriously. American intelligence soon assumed the same view. After running a routine check they downgraded their estimate of his importance.

Yoshikawa spent a great deal of time touring Oahu, sightseeing, swimming, walking about and riding taxis and buses. He also began squandering long and merry evenings in teahouses, particularly one with an excellent view over Pearl Harbor and Hickam Field. He recorded in his memory the smallest details about anything he considered important for his after-midnight summary-reports to Consul-General Kita. For the most part, the two men communicated by writing notes that, once read and understood, were burned immediately.

The ships forming the task force for the raid on Pearl Harbor slipped out of several different ports in Japan in mid-November and sailed northward in blackout and radio silence.

Elaborate steps had been taken to disguise the flotilla's goal. Gear for both foul and tropic weather had been issued to crews in order to confound speculation about destinations. The largest possible number of men left behind were given shore leave so that the absence of others would not be noticeable. False radio traffic around Japan was built up so that no decrease in activity would be evident. Extra flights over civilian areas were made in order that the usual pattern of air traffic would appear to be unchanged. The fleet's call letters were altered to confuse any foreigners who might be listening.

The task force's rendezvous was Hitokappu Bay in the bleak and fog-shrouded Kurile Islands 1,000 miles north of Tokyo. There, under lowering autumn skies, the greatest war fleet ever assembled waited. To residents of a few tiny fishing villages nearby it must have been an ominous and eerie sight: thirty-one ships, dark ghosts looming out of the eternal mists, seeming to be lifeless, brooding on the black water.

They waited: six carriers, two battleships,

three cruisers, nine destroyers, and vessels of the supply forces—the strongest possible concentration of Japan's naval might. Earlier, twenty-seven big submarines had glided away from Japanese home ports. Five of these carried a single 46-ton midget submarine bolted to their decks. Each of those would accommodate two men and two torpedoes. Their mission was to slip into Pearl Harbor before the air attack, then surface later and make kills of ships the aircraft might miss. Their volunteer crewmen accepted the assignment as being the equivalent of suicide.

Intercept of a MAGIC message from the Japanese foreign minister in Tokyo to his ambassadors in Washington on November 4th, 1941:

"Relations between Japan and the United States have reached the edge and our people are losing confidence in the possibility of ever adjusting them.... Conditions both within and without our Empire are so tense that no longer is procrastination possible.... Both in name and spirit this counter-proposal of ours is, indeed, the last. I want you to know that. If through it we do not reach a quick accord, I am sorry to say the talks will certainly be ruptured. Then indeed, will relations between our two nations be on the brink of chaos. I mean that the success or failure of the pending discussions will have an immense effect on the destiny of the Empire of Japan. In fact, we gamble the fate of our land on the throw of this die.... Our temperance, I can tell you, has not come from weakness, and naturally there is an end to our long suffering. Nay, when it comes to a question of our existence and our honor, when the time comes we will defend them without reckoning the cost. . . . We are making our last possible bargain. . . . "

The spy, Yoshikawa, was doing a first-rate job in Honolulu.

His seemingly aimless wanderings around Oahu, his gregariousness, and the sakè-and-song evenings with teahouse girls all were part of his performance, and he was a gifted pretender. His colleagues thought him an amiable fool and wondered why the consul-general put up with him.

Off the consulate grounds, Yoshikawa played the role of the Typical Japanese Tourist. He traveled mostly in taxis, but never by the same one, and he rarely stayed anywhere for more than a few minutes. Sometimes he carried a camera, but it was merely a prop. He made no notes or sketches, relying on an excellent memory.

An astonishing amount of information about Pearl Harbor was available to anyone at the time, simply for the taking. A set of postcards that could be purchased for a dollar provided a complete aerial panorama of the base. The Navy conducted free sightseeing tours through the installation. A fine view of the whole harbor and the Hickam Field area could be enjoyed from nearby Aiea Heights. Private planes were available for hire at Honolulu's John Rodgers Airport, and Yoshikawa took advantage of this service several times. He made frequent visits to Pearl City, an ambitiously-named small community at the midpoint of Pearl Harbor's inland shores. From there, he could easily observe activities on the Ford Island airstrip. Yoshikawa later claimed that he once swam in the lochs at Pearl in an attempt to determine whether or not submarine nets had been laid. He also said that he posed as a Filipino and got work as a dishwasher at the Pearl Harbor officers' mess. Eavesdropping there was fruitful, but the danger was so extreme that he soon withdrew from the job.

American intelligence services closely watched the goings-on at the Japanese consulate, and Yoshikawa knew that he moved under constant threat of exposure. And he worked alone, for he was experiencing a curious kind of frustration. Hawaii's Japanese population numbered more than 157,000 in 1941, comprising thirty-seven percent of the islands' people. Many held dual citizenship with Japan. But Yoshikawa had not been able to enlist a single one to help him in his mission. (Earlier, a German citizen living in Honolulu had been recruited, but he appears to have been incompetent in everything except extracting his fees). Hawaii's Japanese, Yoshikawa reported, were "distressingly loyal" to the United States.

As his deadline closed in on him, Yoshikawa supplied some 150 reports of varied detail to Japan about the numbers and kinds of ships stationed at Pearl, the times they came in and went out, docking procedures, berthing arrangements, numbers of men serving the fleet, the kinds of armament, locations of coral reefs, and the weather. He also forwarded similar intelligence about Hickam Field adjoining Pearl, and the Army's Wheeler Air Force Base, ten miles north and near the center of Oahu.

On November 1st, a steward aboard the visiting Japanese liner *Taiyo Maru* paid a visit to the Japanese consulate in Honolulu. In reality, he was a naval intelligence officer. He dropped a ball of crumpled rice paper into the waiting palm of Consul-General Kita. The slip contained a final set of ninety-seven questions for Yoshikawa. The first of these asked, "On what day of the week would the most ships be in Pearl Harbor?"

Yoshikawa did not have to search for an answer.

"Sunday," he replied.

Intercepted MAGIC dispatch from Foreign Minister Shigenori Togo to Ambassador Nomura in Washington, November 22nd:

"It is awfully hard for us to change the date we set . . . . You should know this, however I know you are working hard. Stick to your fixed policy and do your very best. Spare no efforts and try to bring about the solution we desire. There are reasons beyond your ability to guess why we wanted to settle Japanese-American relations by the 25th. But if within the next three or four days you can finish your conversations with the Americans, if the signing can be completed by the 29th (let me write it out for you, twenty-ninth); if we can get an understanding with the Netherlands and Great Britain; if everything can be finished, we have decided to wait until that date. This time we mean it, that the deadline absolutely cannot be changed. After that, things are automatically going to happen."

The long, silent voyage of the Japanese task force to Hawaii began in the dark, on the morning of November 26th.

As yet there had been no final decision to attack Pearl Harbor. For the starting of a war, the permission of the emperor was required by the terms of the Japanese constitution.

In a conference held on November 30th, Prime Minister Hideki Tojo suggested to Emperor Hirohito that war with the United States was absolutely and urgently necessary: "We cannot gain our contentions by diplomatic means," he said. "The United States, Great Britain, the Netherlands and China have increased their military and economic pressure.... We have no recourse."

Further, he stated that Japan would never be in a better position to win a war. The foreign minister, Shigenori Togo, backed him, and the chiefs of the army and navy told Hirohito that his soldiers, airmen and sailors were "burning with desire to give their lives" at the emperor's command. Hirohito was informed also about the planned attack on the U.S.

Talk turned to the negotiations being held in Washington. Someone suggested that one and one half hours before the surprise attack, the Americans should be given notice that diplomatic relations between the two countries were to be broken. Someone else declared that such a length of time would give the Americans too much warning. Finally, the participants decided that thirty minutes should be the interval between a formal declaration of intent and the surprise attack on American forces.

The emperor conceded with misgivings. He signed a document committing Japan to war. The action was ratified by the cabinet on December 2nd. By then, Admiral Nagumo's task force was in the seventh day of its journey to Hawaii.

On the eleventh day, the Japanese task force had safely passed Midway Island.

But Admiral Nagumo remained glum, still apprehensive.

A message—*Niitakayama nobore,* "Climb

Mount Niitaka"—had been received from Admiral Yamamoto in Japan. This was the code signal that negotiations in Washington had failed and war was certain.

Nagumo now had only one bleak alternative to attacking: if his ships were discovered, he could abandon the mission. But, inconceivably, twenty-four hours before it would launch its aircraft at Pearl Harbor, his huge fleet had not been detected. All around it the sea and sky were empty, the horizon showed no movement of scouting Americans. Aboard the carrier-flagship *Akagi,* Minoru Genda and Mitsuo Fuchida checked and rechecked last minute details. On all ships, crewmen and fliers were taut with excitement.

Nagumo had been told, erroneously, that four U.S. carriers were based at Pearl. But later information from the agent Yoshikawa in Honolulu said that none were in the harbor. Nagumo wondered where they could be. Encountering a bee-swarm from a *Lexington* or an *Enterprise* so near their goal would demolish the Japanese plan. Perhaps the Americans knew somehow of his approach and were looking for him . . .

In the meantime he had no choice. His orders from Yamamoto were explicit: hostile actions against the United States were to be commenced on December 7th.

And now his men were listening to Hawaiian music from Honolulu on their radios.

By autumn I had been promoted out of the helper class to journeyman shipfitter. I sent the news pridefully to my father, who took it as some kind of joke or the result of a clerical error, knowing how

UP
Sportswriters
Pick
Yanks To Win

14

Beverly Hills, Calif.—
The much publicized
fisticuffs between
Errol Flynn and columnist
Jimmy Fidler ended
legally today when
Flynn promised a
municipal court
judge that he would-
n't punch Jimmy
any more . . . .

FDR
Sees
Long Hours,
Harsh
Times

15

Editor,
The *Honolulu Advertiser*
Dear Sir:
It's about time
that the great major-
ity of Americans
stopped kidding them-
selves about this man
named Adolf Hitler . . . .

16

World Close To Ruin Says Jewish Chaplain

"The Government is spending about $1 billion on Hawaii, together with the far Pacific Bases, and when the entire program is completed, no navy in the world will be able to penetrate our western defenses."
—Rep. James E. Van Zandt of Pennsylvania, who visited Honolulu in October, 1941

RAY ROBINSON
DECISIONS ZIVIC

Harlem Youngster Gives
Ex-champ Thrashing

Japanese Navy Hinted Active

No Reason For Alarm, U.S. Authorities Say

Al Capone is unhappy, those taxes again....
—Walter Winchell

Only 39
Shopping Days
Until Christmas

Rats Devour Draft Records At Kaimuki

18

DIMAGGIO
SELECTED
MOST
VALUABLE
PLAYER

Fred Allen
Returns As
Information
Please
Guest

Craig Wood
is captain of the Ryder
Cup Team. Jimmy
Demaret, Vic Ghezzi, Ben
Hogan, Lloyd Mangrum,
Jug McSpaden, Byron
Nelson, Gene Sarazen,
Sam Snead and Horton
Smith are . . . .

19   20

21
22

**Dorothy Thompson
Sues
Sinclair Lewis
For Divorce**

23

Washington Sees Little Hope of Relaxing Pacific Tension

Kurusu's Visit Stall For Time, Observers Say

24

The Green Hornet comes very close to having his identity revealed in next Thursday's episode of the popular KGU mystery thriller. . . .

25

Severe Earthquake Rocks Los Angeles

"The new Kapiolani Boulevard could, in a pinch, be used as an airplane runway. It might be necessary to remove a few trees . . . but that could be done in a pinch too."
—*Paradise of the Pacific,* November

26

**New Telephone
Service Set
For Pearl Harbor**

SARNOFF SEES MAN "BURSTING BONDS OF TOIL"

"... Uranium has been discovered, which may lead to the smashing of the atom, which will release incredible sources of power.... The day is not too far distant when we will be able to see through television as far as we can now hear through radio...."

Editor,
The Honolulu Advertiser

Dear Sir:

It is difficult for me to understand how a flyer, flying almost low enough to hit the roof of a house where his brother officers are having a party, is carrying out Defense Training. Likewise, the lads who drop billet doux on their ladies in congested districts. In the States the other day a civilian house was hit. Why should Honolulu and its rural districts be different?

Out and Out American

A PRETTY NEW STARLET
for Hollywood is Ava Gardner, who smiles for the camera after her contract was ....

27

28

Kurusu
Demands
U.S.
Ease
Economic
Hold

" ... thousands of men and women, new to
Hawaii, new to the life of Hawaii, have
swarmed into the city.... New cities have
sprung up in the suburbs of Honolulu, at
Wheeler Field, Pearl Harbor, Hickam Field
.... Life here teems with new personalities,
new enterprises, new demands, all new to
Hawaii. The old, we fear, has gone, never to
return."

—*Paradise of the Pacific*, November-December, 1941

unaccomplished a "mechanic" I was. My mother
relayed his observation that the U.S. Navy was in a
helluva lot of trouble if they depended on the
likes of me to fix their ships.

October waned in a summer sameness.
And more men arrived, from Bremerton and
Brooklyn, California and Alaska. The huge new
Shop 11 for shipfitters neared completion, large
enough to contain ten of the old structure. The
drydock and repair basin reeked of boiling tar and
burning metal. There were litters of wood chips
and tin scraps, snarls everywhere of hawsers and
hoses, and always the noise, the tooth-rattling
tattoos of riveters and chippers, the sledgehammer
blows ringing against resistant steel.

The villain who ran the Yard Cafeteria was
unable to house the noontime horde. He acquired
satellite lunchwagons and wheeled them near
the larger jobs. In blazing noon we bought his
soggy sandwiches and tepid coffee, found friends
and sought shade near tool sheds or under cranes.
Older men talked of lean years and hard times.
The Depression decade was a vivid memory, its
wounds unhealed, the fears lingering. For us
younger chaps the lunchtime salons ran the spectrum of books, girls, music and movies. We
indulged in aimless argument and dipped our toes
into shallows of philosophy. It was inconceivable
that those sad experiences of the older men
could ever happen to us. And events in a larger
world were outlandish maneuverings, hardly
noticed. Our detachment was complete, the
splendid, innocent insulation of the young.

We worked on worlds large and small, metal microcosms with many shapes named *Shaw, Lexington, Kukui, Baltimore, Enterprise, Rigel, Condor* and *California.* The bigger vessels, the battleships and carriers, were monsters of impersonality at first. They were like cities afloat, come to visit, gargantuan sculptures dwarfing all buildings along the harbor's entrance, imperious presences sliding to berths at Ford Island's Battleship Row or along Ten-Ten Dock. But as they neared shore, strings of bright pennants fluttered up. Rumblings of screws and the pipings of bosun's whistles were heard. Specks of white became sailors scurrying into formations under huge guns or on spacious flight decks.

Secured, engines stilled, the ships became sharp silhouettes against the bleached sky and gentle greens of foothills. And we poured aboard to begin our attacks with hammers, drills, saws and torches, losing ourselves in deep puzzles of passageways, walking wide-eyed over flight decks the size of football fields. Often we were lifted, fearful and clutching at lines, to dizzy heights in the superstructure, to fit brackets for the new gear called radar. Other kinds of mysterious equipment needed installing in Combat Intelligence rooms—and always the familiar pom-poms and 20-millimeter anti-aircraft guns were arriving for mounting.

Among the crews of destroyers, minesweepers and other smaller ships there was a tendency to informality. But on the big vessels there was a detachment, an aloofness, and we moved and worked uneasily under the stares of crotchety petty officers and gold-braided senior men. Immaculate and steel-stiff marines guarded tightly dogged hatches. Gangway details snapped to quivering attention when admirals were piped aboard. In spotless wardrooms, signal bridges and deck areas the crewmen watched us with pure distaste. Our coming meant assault upon their beloved mistress; our gouging, ripping and burning was a kind of rape; it brought sacrilege to surroundings they had polished, again and again, to brightest gleam and proudest face.

Smoke plumed to disappear in the trade-winds. Welders sparked light so intense that it smashed through sunshine. Stifflegged cranes traveled along the piers and drydock like immense iron birds, their beaks dangling guns, boxes and boilers. Often one carried a rigger, high and swaying with his foot in a hook, free hand signalling, supremely contemptuous of earthbound workers below.

Ex-sailors and Hawaiians made the best riggers, men who had been long wed to the sea, who moved easily in high places, were calmly efficient with blocks and tackle, cool in times of danger. Often I paused to watch them lead a ship into drydock, easing the great vessel into the coffinful of water with shouts, arm and fist signals, and the play of heavy line drawn from sag to taut. The thick hempen hawsers choked incredibly tight around the black iron chocks, snapping spray, squeezing out water as if wrung from rags and whining protest at the strain. The leathery men worked the lines with delicacy, cursing and coaxing, giving and taking first yards, then feet, then inches. It was always a wonder to me, when the dock was finally emptied of its water, to see how the mighty hulls sat magically in air, their keels laid precisely across the centers of big wooden blocks on the drydock's floor.

Then the longer scene was played out. Goggled laborers descended sides of the drydock to clean the barnacled bottoms of the ships. Topside, the gangplanks bowed under the weight of workers and equipment. Canvas tubes snaked out from blowers forcing air into the deeper and darker places needing repair. Power lines supplying burners, welders and chippers festooned the ship's side and decks. Fire watchers from the ship's crew sat beside their red CO_2 bottles. Bored and sulky, they listened as blaring loudspeakers dismissed liberty parties of thirsting and coltish comrades.

For days and even weeks the patient ships dripped their multiple umbilicals of hose, cable and line. And now lights burned all night in the drydock and repair basin. A swing shift had been put on in most crafts from late afternoon to midnight. Then a smaller, "graveyard" gang took over until morning brought another day. Soon it would be Thanksgiving, then Christmastime. Those of us left out of the arrivals on the *Wash-ington* had been in Hawaii a year. In November I was moved, with two or three other shipfitters, to the swing-shift. Our job was to build a new yard-tugboat on the pier, right under the hammerhead crane.

In Waikiki, our landlady, The Widow, began

escalating a hobby to accompany her Bing Crosby records and chain-store gin. Now she was entertaining members of the armed forces nightly, without prejudice to rank or age. The revelry became much too spirited for us. Noland moved nearer to his girl's house, and I rented refuge in a clutch of decrepit cottages near the beach and Kapiolani Park. Many Hawaiians and other types of local folk lived there in a loose Polynesian style, and the decibel count of our nights was lower. The place was called the Lalani Village. Doors were always open and iceboxes and kitchens were communal.

The elderly owner of the Village was dedicated to remaining as Hawaiian as time's march and a growing parade of strangers permitted. He was always eager to talk about the old culture to anyone who would listen. Sadly, few people found the time, even among his fellow aboriginals, and I still have a mental film of the white-haired old chap puttering about his grounds, trying to corner an audience for his perplexing rambles about the genealogies of chiefs long dead, or the sad end to the Hawaiian monarchy.

Yet he too had been infected by the changes. On weekends he created a modest profit by staging public luaus. Tables composed of bright green ti leaves were set on the turf, and a small platform was moved in for dancers and musicians to use. For a few hours all this was very pleasant: the sweet voices lifted in lyric explorations, the guitars pulsing, the swishing of ti-leaf hula skirts—and the frequent chuckles as the musicians inserted bawdy ad-libs into their songs that only their brother Hawaiians understood.

But after the paying guests had returned to homes or hotel rooms, the party would take on an entirely different personality. The musicians began playing for themselves and other Hawaiians. Songs became unfamiliar, often plaintive. Listeners' thoughts turned inward and faces of people who sat on the grass grew pensive. Older folk rose to dance and sing less familiar melodies, chants about families lost, or lagoons abandoned and valleys long deserted. The invaders have won, their voices seemed to say—we are at the end of our line. A far deeper meaning entered into the traditional words so often used to signal the end of an Island song:

"Haina ia mai, ana kapuana . . . ": "Now I come to the end of my story . . . "

The day came when our new Yard Tug was hoisted by the hammerhead crane and lowered tenderly into the bay. She was a pretty sight, buoyant and perky, looking very special to us despite her small size and unfinished topside. Most of her hull work was complete and she was given over to machinists, electricians, painters and other workers for final outfitting and cosmetic attention.

I was sent back to the day shift in early December. Dave Melville was my boss, an oldtime steelworker, pug-faced and fatherly. Our group loitered in the sun, watching while Drydock One was emptied. The destroyers *Cassin* and *Downes* had been worked in, followed by the fleet's flagship-battleship, *Pennsylvania*. Men on decks and bridges of the ships stared down as riggers played out lines, water was withdrawn, and the ships settled to rest.

Dave assigned us to tasks on the destroyers, the *Downes* first. Both she and the *Cassin* were new, twins of 1935-36 construction. But the hullplates in their bow sections had not proved to be heavy enough for strong seas. Our job was to replace several plates on each side with thicker steel. I don't think we even had a blueprint to follow. Dave made rough sketches, then we waited while scaffolds were erected and equipment and power hoses were dropped down. In the bright sunshine the dock floor dried quickly. Knots of workmen sat smoking and waiting in shadier places. When the fo'c'sle was emptied of its crew, chalk lines were snapped on the ship's side and these were counterpunched, dimpling the steel for the burner's cuts. The men held their torches like billiard cues and bent to work, a cruel surgery upon the ship's sleekness. When their arrow tips of flame cut through the ship's skin, muffled cries and curses came from fire-watchers inside, suddenly showered with the molten rain.

Other sounds clamored incessantly— cranes clacking, bullhorns blaring and carpenters rapping. Bells, whistles and shouting bosses punctuated the din.

But beyond these nests of noise Pearl Harbor was still miles of placidity, shining like pewter left in sun, or crinkled by breezes, and all rimmed with green in freshest hues. The sky was the clearest and cleanest blue, except for the cottony clouds that hovered to windward, above deep valley walls of the Koolaus.

Little pressures began nagging our elderly Hawaiian landlord.

Rumor had it that a big money interest wanted ownership or control of his "village." We heard whisperings about the compound being razed for new houses . . . The cottages were firetraps . . . And the old wheeze, warning that if the termites stopped holding hands someone would get hurt.

There was also talk about a new hotel. The rickety shacks sat on very valuable land, only twenty yards or so away from the famed waters of Waikiki. More and more tourists were visiting the islands. Even the Clipper planes were full on their weekly flights. At times, Honolulu's three existing beach hotels were hard pressed to house all the business. Obviously, in a heightening visitor-economy, this attractive acreage should not be wasted by Hawaiians in mere living.

Apparently the dazed old proprietor surrendered. He went away—to one of the neighbor islands, we heard. The songs and dancing stopped.

Chilly-eyed strangers soon appeared, talking politely about making changes and raising rents. This was a gloomy prospect to blithe souls in residence who had trouble enough raising the current damage. The village's dwellers trickled off in various directions. Windows went blank. One by one the doors swung open on emptiness. I moved across the Ala Wai canal to share a small house with a machinist named Al Sharkay.

PART THREE

FLAME

"It is terrible to think this is God's will."
—Admiral Isoroku Yamamoto

Often on Saturdays I went into Honolulu to stroll, shop, and stare, sometimes with friends but frequently alone.

A regular destination was the musty book-store for new and used publications on Nuuanu Avenue. Its walls sagged with overstuffed shelves, and a small mezzanine creaked under the weight of volumes and browsing customers. An ex-soldier named Joe Herwig owned the shop and dearly loved his wares. Large-nosed and forever hitching up his pants, Joe could talk knowledgeably about any one of the thousands of items crammed into his establishment. He also understood that he was in business for profit. A crate handy to the cash register was always filled with the works of Cald-well, Cain, Farrell, Bocaccio, and bootleg Henry Miller—highly desired spice in those days for bland nights at sea or in the barracks.

Outside, streets thronged with townsfolk and transients. Sailors, soldiers and defense workers swarmed on narrow sidewalks, moving in and out of curio shops, amusement parlors and cafes. Servicemen freed for the day, euphoric on liquor and release, spilled from Bill Lederer's, Hoffman's, the Rialto and the Two Jacks. More

gaiety awaited at Moose Taussig's Pantheon on
Nuuanu, the oldest saloon in Honolulu, its bar a
large and intricately carved expanse of wood
shipped to the islands in King Kalakaua's day.
During the 1880s, the Merry Monarch himself had
tippled and played poker at the Pantheon with
Hawaii's merchant and social princes. But in 1941,
Moose ran it as a rendezvous for sports lovers
and fight fans. Its stained-glass swinging doors
flapped constantly, and a punch-drunk pug shined
shoes and made unreliable book in a niche off the
sidewalk. Day and night, Moose played happy host
to boxers and ballplayers, gamblers, sycophants,
sporting girls, and casuals.

A few doors away, yet still in the middle of
this spirited bacchanal, the bookshop beckoned,
a shoal of quiet culture in a river of revelry. Inside
its narrow door a seeker could find cool peace, and
the warm glow of pleasure in the rustling of pages
and sparkle of book-talk. It was a place of contrasts
not only in inventory but in patronage. Hookers,
seamen, judges, professors, and we ordinary
worker bibliophiles bumped each other in the
dusky aisles, usually smiling and invariably polite.
Herwig's haven also attracted the inevitable off-
beat itinerants. Once I chanced upon a Hawaiian
girl nursing her baby in one of those quiet alcoves.
She was swaying, crooning to the suckling infant,
her ebony eyes lowered in a mother's happiness.

Hawaii has no seasons. There are only
the times that are less gentle than others. Thinking
back, so many fragments of memory return to me:
tender hours of morning and flowers, walking barefoot upon cornmeal sand in the warm caress of
rain, moving through days of unforgettable

discovery. And the loveliness of that little island madonna in the bookshop.

That Saturday would have been like any other. Nothing of any importance marked it. The sun came up and traveled over the islands and people moved about in all their ordinary and complacent ways. It was a day without distinction, merely December 6th, 1941.

For thirty-five years now I have heard many vivid recollections from people about where they were and exactly what they were doing when Pearl Harbor was attacked. But I have never heard anyone mention what they were doing the day before. It was simply a Saturday, nothing of significance set it apart.

Honolulu newspapers for that day noted coming Christmas events, community activities for servicemen and club news. The big sporting event was a football match at the Honolulu Stadium between the University of Hawaii and Willamette. *A Yank In The RAF*, starring Betty Grable and Tyrone Power, was playing at the Waikiki Theater, and the Royal Hawaiian Band announced its usual Sunday concert under the ironwoods at Kapiolani Park.

Navy Commander Charles Momsen, inventor of the submariner's "lung" and rescue chamber, spoke to Honolulu's Commercial Club. Over on Kauai, editorial writer and radio commentator William Ewing addressed a gathering of the Mokihana Society. Ewing criticized FDR's handling of labor problems, but said he would much rather see the president make mistakes with

John L. Lewis than with Saburo Kurusu or
Adolf Hitler.

In "News Around The Territory," one
read that Mrs. Goonki Furukawa had been elected
president of the Wailuku Japanese Christian
Ladies Aid Society on Maui. On the Big Island of
Hawaii, Kohala Girl Reserves and HiYs cele-
brated a joint candlelight ceremony. At Hamakua,
an oratorical contest was held at the Kukaiau
Japanese School by the young people's association.
Patriotism was the theme and speeches were made
in Japanese and English.

On Oahu, Abraham John Kalaokahaku
Kaimana, a retired fish inspector and school
teacher, died at age seventy. Kaimana was
widowed and a Mormon. Young Whan Kim, too,
was dead, at age fifty-five. He was a retired plantation laborer, and services for him were held at the
Korean Christian Church. Births were reported
into families named Ludewig, Fukao, Kahoonei,
Vierra, Hookano, Hoogs, Hales, Robello, and
Elisary. The listing ran the gamut of Hawaii's racial
potpourri and was not at all unusual.

Advertisements in the *Star Bulletin* and in
the *Advertiser* offered cellophane Christmas
wreaths at twenty-five cents each, and new console
radio-phonographs for $127. Tun Chun Tong
bought space to announce the addition of hard
liquors to his regular features of soft drinks,
magazines and Chinese herbs. Theo H. Davies &
Company's fifty-dollar U.S. Savings Bond Award
went to Corporal Harry Dittmer, Jr., of Fort
Shafter. Dittmer had written copy advancing the
idea that football and democracy similarly defined
true Americanism.

It was a time for such observations. A picture of beaming, plump-cheeked George Akita ran above a story about his winning first prize of ten dollars in the D.A.R. oratory contest. George was fifteen years old, and part of his speech went: "From tropical Hawaii to the rock-bound shores of Maine, to the snow-clad plains of the Dakotas to sunny Texas, let us, Americans all, rally round the Stars and Stripes in the defense of our way of life. With the love of democracy burning in our hearts and minds we cannot fail—we must not fail!"

Another American-Japanese youngster, Terue Masatsuga, took second place with her address, "A United America." Third place went to Colin Kippen for his "Americanism vs. Radicalism."

In Saturday's weather news, a chill 46 degrees had been the low for the week. But that was recorded almost two hundred miles away from Honolulu, thousands of feet up on the stony flanks of Mauna Loa on the Big Island. For Honolulu, the forecast was "Clear, with occasional mauka showers drifting makai." Translated, this meant balmy loveliness, with rainbow-bearing mists floating down from the Koolau peaks toward the leeward shorelines. The identical forecast was valid for almost every day of the year on Oahu.

So, undoubtedly, it was a day of pearlshell clouds touched with violet and gold, a day of tradewinds flecking whitecaps over channels between the islands. Twilight lingered for a brief while, the horizon fire died, and its last light threw long and final shadows before the sea and sky became one.

The Saturday night ceremonies were underway.

Downtown shops remained open longer. Hotel Street bars, and tattoo, massage and pinball parlors did a thriving business. Waiting rooms in the River Street whorehouses were filled with patrons self-consciously ignoring each other and smoking nervously. "Tantalizing Tootsies," a variety show at the Princess Theater, played to a large audience. The mass of servicemen would return to bases or barracks before midnight, but some would stay in town. The shore patrol and Honolulu police had a quiet night, despite the thousands of men on liberty.

Many Honoluluans dressed for dinner at the Young Hotel, the Royal Hawaiian, or Lau Yee Chai's. The Waikiki Tavern filled early with drinkers and diners. As on all weekend nights, many private parties sprang to life. On hillsides, along beach lanes and in valleys, luau torches fueled with kerosene flickered in front of homes— the traditional island signal that a party was in progress. There were family gatherings for birthdays and wedding anniversaries. And parties given without any reason at all. Saturday nights were for letting a good time feed itself with beer, talk and laughter, songs and dances.

On lonely shores, eternally optimistic surfcasters set rods in holders, hoping their reels would screech excitement in the night. There were campfires on the beaches at Nanakuli, Haleiwa, and Kailua. Families grilled steaks and hamburgers over hibachis at Kapiolani Park. Highrolling gamblers began their professional play in guarded rooms downtown, and waiters juggled trays of steaming food at Wo Fat's, the Honolulu Cafe, and Kaimuki Inn.

At Hickam, Kaneohe, Wheeler, Schofield, DeRussy and Ruger, military service clubs leaped alive in their popular Saturday night specials of dinner, drink and dancing. Slot machines thumped and bars rattled with business. At Bloch Center near the Pearl Harbor gate a "Battle of Bands" attracted an enthusiastic crowd from the fleet. Bloch was new, the enlisted man's gathering place for beer, boxing shows, poolshooting, and other recreation. The battle of music featured groups from the *Pennsylvania, Tennessee, Argonne* and *Detroit*.

The two top military commanders in Hawaii were attending parties. Neither affair could be described as swinging. Lt. General Walter C. Short went to dinner with colleagues at the Schofield Officers Club and left for return to his quarters on the same post at 9:30 p.m. Rear Admiral Husband E. Kimmel joined friends at the Halekulani Hotel in Waikiki, sipped his usual token drink, dined, and left early enough to be home and in bed before ten.

The day had not been an ordinary one for either man. Of late, none of their days could be considered as routine. There had been a secret warning from Washington that the Japanese would soon strike—possibly at the Philippines, or Borneo, or the Thai Peninsula—no one really knew. Hawaii was not mentioned, but General Short was chronically worried about possible sabotage from local Japanese in the event of aggression by Japan. The Honolulu FBI had monitored a telephone call to Tokyo on the previous day, with much superfluous, suspicious talk about island flowers being in bloom. Short had alerted his command and ordered planes on all Army airfields lined up neatly, under guards, to minimize danger.

Admiral Kimmel had many things on his mind. Both his fleet and his responsibilities had been expanding immensely. He was a proud and serious man who had been jumped over thirty other admirals into this command. He knew the Japanese aircraft carriers had disappeared somewhere into the Pacific. His own carriers were at sea under Admiral William Halsey, the *Enterprise* carrying planes to Wake Island, the *Lexington* on a similar mission to Midway. His eight battleships were moored snugly for the weekend along Ford Island.

Kimmel and Short had a great deal to talk about. And would. They had a date to play golf, first thing Sunday morning.

I had to work on that Saturday night.

In Drydock One, the *Downes* had gaping rectangular openings in her bow, ready to receive the new plates. To finish the destroyer was a priority job and some of us had been moved to the swing shift to hasten the work. The *Cassin*, alongside, would be started when the *Downes* was sealed. The destroyer twins were perched parallel on the drydock floor, looking small under the soaring bow of the *Pennsylvania*.

We were briefed by men going off shift. There was a little cleaning up to be done, they said, but the new steel was on the way from the shop and we could start hanging it. Our strawboss was Caesar Paishon, a gruff, no-nonsense Portuguese-Hawaiian, and soon we were at work.

When we came back from supper, I
remember how the drydock looked like a dozing
volcano, its rim sharp against the glow of lights
deep inside. The superstructure of the
Pennsylvania was a towering vagueness, looming
high over the smaller vessels. She was like a
mother at rest in that concrete chamber, with her
destroyer-children safely tucked in for the night. In
the mealtime pause music could be heard: Glenn
Miller's reedy "Moonlight Serenade," Artie Shaw's
clarinet in "Moonglow."

Their moods were smashed when work
resumed. Cranes dropped the new plates down to
us and we fought them into place with crowbars
and sledgehammer blows. Welders made blinding
contact, and bright streams of molten metal cascaded
down to bounce off the drydock floor. The intense
blue-white light sent great shadows dancing upon
the dock's walls. The air was almost still, and
smoke gathered in the low pocket until it was
oppressive. Frequently we had to wait for the haze
to rise and be blown away. During a break I went
inside the *Downes* to cadge some coffee.

A chief bosun's mate had the duty and we
sat in the chief petty officers' quarters drinking a
thick brew. He was addressing Christmas cards,
with troubled pauses, his brow furrowed and pen
poised. He said he was writing the same goddam
thing on all the goddam cards, and asked me for
ideas. I remember teaching him how to spell Merry
Christmas in Hawaiian, "Mele Kalikimaka."
Then the burners resumed their cutting, and the
sick-sweet fumes from burning galvanized iron
rose in the compartment. We went topside for a
bit of fresh air.

On the bridge a sailor on firewatch griped
to the chief about drawing the duty on a Saturday
night. The chief told him, quite cordially I recall,
to go fuck himself. The *Cassin* alongside was nearly
dark. Most of her crew were ashore. But the chief
waved over to someone he knew and they shouted
jolly obscenities back and forth.

We stood there for awhile, smoking and
watching laborers underneath the *Pennsylvania.*
They were like a platoon of ghosts with goggles
and rags around their heads and wearing cocoon-
like coveralls. Theirs was ugly work, sandblasting
the crusted bottoms. The battleship's bow was a
huge spade-shape above our heads. Her upper
decks forward were quiet, but there were stirrings
and lights farther aft. Beyond the drydock, along
Ten-Ten Dock, the lights of the *Helena* were showing. Across the water, off Ford Island, we could see
twinklings from the *Avocet, Neosha,* and *California* and beyond, the beady lights of other battleships. The destroyer *Shaw* and tug *Sotoyomo*
presented only a small scattering of lights in the
floating drydock. The chief said the whole fleet
was in, except he hadn't seen any carriers lately.
It was a lovely night, with stars pricking the
infinite vault above, and air turning cool as time
moved toward midnight.

We went back below. The chief had
given up on his Christmas cards, muttering about
goddam smoke and goddam noise. He was going to
try to get some goddam sleep.

I remember nothing else about those last
few hours before the war began. Perhaps because
they had the sameness of other nights: quitting
work around midnight, taking a quick scrub and

change in the locker room, and joining friends for the ride home. More than likely we went to the Kau Kau Korner drive-in for our usual hamburger and useless flirtations with the carhops. Then we would have gone home and to bed.

TOWARD FOUR O'CLOCK that Sunday morning a watch officer on the minesweeper *Condor* had spotted a strange object in the dark waters off Pearl Harbor. Using binoculars, he determined that it was the conning tower of a small submarine, moving about 1,000 yards off the harbor entrance. American submarines were expressly forbidden to operate in that area. This mysterious craft had no business being there.

Condor blinked a message to the nearby destroyer *Ward* that a partly submerged sub had been sighted, cruising on a westerly course at nine knots.

The commander of the *Ward* was aroused and ordered general quarters. His ship patrolled back and forth but saw nothing. At 4:45 most of the crew went back to their bunks. The incident was not reported. Fifteen minutes later the harbor's boom gate was opened and the minesweeper *Crossbill* passed into the channel. The gate was left open for a tugboat scheduled to go out to sea soon after. It is assumed that two Japanese midget submarines entered Pearl Harbor during this interval.

But another still lurked in the neighborhood. At about 6:30 the *Ward's* watch saw a periscope following behind the supply ship *Antares*. The destroyer closed in to less than a hundred yards and opened fire. The second shell hit the sub's conning tower at the waterline. Four depth-charges were dropped as the submarine twisted about in the *Ward's* wake.

At 6:53 the captain of the destroyer reported the encounter to 14th Naval District Headquarters. Time sped by while the communication was decoded and typed. More time elapsed while it was discussed and moved on its slow way up the chain of command. Admiral Kimmel received the message by telephone at 7:40. In exactly fifteen minutes his world would explode and his career would be shattered.

At 5:50 a.m. the six Japanese carriers had idled their engines and were wallowing deep in troughs of the waves. High seas smashed against dipping bows. The armada lay 220 miles north of Oahu, and, according to latest intelligence, apparently the Americans were unaware that anything unusual was going on anywhere in the Pacific. No barrage balloons had been sent up over Pearl Harbor and the battleships were moored quietly along Ford Island. Twenty minutes earlier the Japanese had launched two seaplanes to make a final scouting, but their reports would not be available to Admiral Nagumo for more than an hour.

Now breakfast was finished, final briefings were given, and calculations concerning wind, distance and time were studied and committed to memory. Prayers to the gods had been offered before Shinto shrines in the ships. Pilots sat tensely in their planes waiting for flags on the *Akagi* to flutter up, signaling their release. Goodbyes had been said, some with emotion, others elaborately casual. Bows had been exchanged and last touchings made. Most of the airmen wore white headbands, inscribed with characters signifying their willingness to die for the emperor. Their mission was holy, the excitement intense.

The flattops swung into the wind. The *Akagi's*

signal flags rose and fell. Shouts of banzais from the watching crews were lost in the roars of revving motors. At six o'clock, Mitsuo Fuchida led the first wave of 183 planes, hurtling off the carriers' decks. The most deadly gathering of air power ever assembled droned toward a sleeping Oahu.

Fuchida later wrote:

"We flew through and over the thick clouds which were at 2,000 meters, up to where the day was ready to dawn. And the clouds began to brighten below us....

At 0700 I figured that we should reach Oahu in less than an hour. But flying over the clouds we could not see the surface of the water, and, consequently, had no check on our drift. I switched on the radio direction-finder to tune in the Honolulu radio station and soon picked up some light music.... I found the exact direction from which the broadcast was coming and corrected our course, which had been five degrees off....

I was wondering how to get below the clouds after reaching Oahu. If the island was covered by thick clouds like those below us, the level bombing would be difficult, and we had not yet had reports from the reconnaissance planes.

In tuning the radio a little finer, I heard, along with the music, what seemed to be a weather report. Holding my breath, I adjusted the dial and listened intently. Then I heard it come through a second time, slowly and distinctly: 'Averaging partly cloudy with clouds mostly over the mountains ... visibility good. Wind north, 10 knots.'

What a windfall for us!"

Army privates George Elliot and Joseph Lockard manned a radar station on the remote northern coast of Oahu. Their mobile equipment was one of five stations located on the perimeter of the island, and the two young soldiers commuted to duty from a small camp nine miles away.

Near 7 a.m. on Sunday the parent station at Fort Shafter told them they could start closing down. A few minutes earlier on their screen they had spotted two aircraft coming in from the northwest, but this was not an unusual event. Because both men were quite interested in their jobs on the fairly new gear, they decided to keep the set going until a truck arrived to take them back to camp for breakfast.

Elliot was scanning the screen when the big blip appeared, bigger than anything they'd ever seen before. He and Lockard, equally puzzled, first ran a check on the equipment but nothing was wrong with it. The radar clearly showed a big flight of aircraft moving toward Oahu. At 7:10 they telephoned Fort Shafter with the information that a rather large number of planes were approaching the island from the north.

The young lieutenant at Fort Shafter was in command of the central post for the first time, as part of his training duty. He thought a few moments, then decided that the planes must be coming from American carriers at sea, or perhaps were patrols from Hickam Field—or even the flight of B-17s that was due to arrive soon from the West Coast.

He told Lockard and Elliot not to worry, to forget it.

At 7:45 their truck arrived and they locked up the unit and went off to breakfast.

The planes arrowed in over a deserted ocean, with the sun rising to meet them.

They crossed over Oahu's shoreline at 10,000 feet, Fuchida in the lead with fifty high-level bombers. On his right and left were squadrons of equal size. One group was loaded with armor-piercing bombs, and the other, made up of "Kate" dive-bombers, was equipped with torpedos slung under their bellies. High above, forty-three Zero fighters flew in escort.

On Fuchida's signal, the dive bombers lifted themselves to 15,000 feet, then broke into two groups. One aimed for the army's Wheeler Field in central Oahu, the other for Ford Island and Hickam Field. The Kates swung seaward, beginning a turn that would bring them back upon Pearl Harbor from the south.

The scattering of ships on the lake-still waters of Pearl Harbor seemed to be without life. A few cars crawled among buildings in the shipyard. The highway aiming from Honolulu was almost bare of traffic.

To the Japanese, the sight of the lovely island dozing in sabbath, and the sounds of lilting Hawaiian music on the radio were almost beyond believing. Fuchida said later: "Below me lay the whole Pacific Fleet in a formation I would not have dared dream. I have never seen ships even in the deepest peace anchored less than 500 yards from each other. .... The picture was difficult to comprehend."

At 7:49 he signalled for the attack to begin. His radio operator tapped out the first syllable of the Japanese word for attack: "To ... To ... To ..."

Aboard his flagship, in Japan's Inland Sea, Admiral Yamamoto stared at a clock and listened to a radio. Five minutes later, helped by an atmospheric fluke, he heard Fuchida broadcast the Japanese word for tiger, the code word telling that complete surprise had been achieved.

"Tora ... Tora ... Tora ... "

Admiral Yamamoto, according to reports, heard the news without a show of emotion.

It was a complete surprise everywhere.

Within minutes, the low-flying Kates were nearing their targets in the lochs at Pearl. The dive-bombers were whistling down on Oahu's airfields. The Zeros, assigned to engage American aircraft, met none and joined the other planes to strafe at will.

At Hickam Field, some seventy aircraft, including twelve of the new "Flying Fortresses," sat like toys on display. In moments the quiet field became an insane nightmare. The same scenario for disaster was played out at other airfields, where planes were lined up in precise rows before hangars. Deafening explosions racked Wheeler air base among the pineapple plantations; Kaneohe, on the sheltered shores of windward Oahu; Ford Island; and even the new airfield at Ewa to the west of Pearl. The trapped planes burst into flames, barracks and hangers exploded and burned, hundreds of men were almost instantly killed. Within a few minutes, U.S. airpower in the central Pacific had been ruthlessly smashed.

At almost the same time, Japan's torpedo bombers, descending almost to sea level, aimed their noses at the battleships lined up along the eastern shore of Ford Island. The attack had started at 7:55, and they began their runs to the slaughter just after eight. Each bomber had a 1,760-pound torpedo clutched to its belly and each pilot had been given a special target. The Kates dipped down, to their final mile of straight run at the sleeping giants on Battleship Row.

It was so easy, the pilots said later.

Easier even than the practice runs they'd made at Kagoshima.

From 15,000 feet in the air, Fuchida watched.

In the first torpedo attack the *California, Oklahoma* and *West Virginia* had been struck. In the second, the *Helena* and *Oglala*. The *Raleigh* and the *Utah* took two torpedos each.

Then the dive bombers went in. They made eight separate attacks from different directions.

The most shattering hit was on the *Arizona,* igniting her forward magazines and killing more than a thousand men. The old dreadnought was ripped to pieces. The explosion was so great that it blew men off the decks of neighboring ships. The concussion stopped vehicles moving on Ford Island and caused Japanese planes in the air high above to tremble.

Soon the time came for Fuchida to bring his high-level bombers into action. Forty-nine planes, six hundred feet apart, formed a column for the assault. He had instructed his crews to make as many passes as necessary to score bullseye hits. By now, puffs of smoke from anti-aircraft fire flecked the sky, but his men flew straight into the flak. Pilots unable to see their targets through the billowing smoke nearer the ground circled back for second and third attempts. Fuchida himself made three runs before dropping his bombs, then he lifted up his plane, to assess the damage below.

Pearl Harbor was a cauldron of dying men and

**blazing ships. And the attack had begun less than an
hour before.**

A sailor I knew on the *Utah*, Van was his name,
told me he was up early that morning. A shipmate
woke him for breakfast and he ate heartily, then
went topside.

It was a pretty morning, Sunday-quiet,
with cloudrolls nuzzling the mountains and sun
beginning to warm the day. He climbed to the
signal bridge, to drink coffee and chat with friends.
The *Utah* was a retired battleship, in service only
as a target vessel. Her deck had been covered with
concrete and most of her structures were enclosed
in boxlike protective constructions. The crew was
small and her men knew each other. Van said he
bullshitted with his mates, killing time until he was
due to relieve the supervisory watch at 8 o'clock.

The ship's colors were being readied for
hoisting when three planes came in low and from
the south. The men watched, idly curious about
who was flying at that odd hour. Then the planes
dropped some objects upon the other side of Ford
Island, in the battleship anchorage. A moment
later they heard explosions. Van said they were
struck dumb. He thought this must be some awful
mistake, or an air drill. He and his mates stared
at one another.

He went to the port side and saw more
planes coming in from that direction, and then
from every direction, and he saw the emblem of
the rising sun on their wings. Spellbound, he
watched as several bombers came in low, heading
straight for his ship. There were splashes in the

131

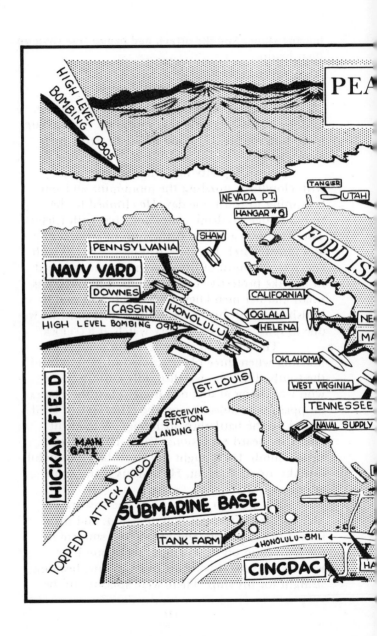

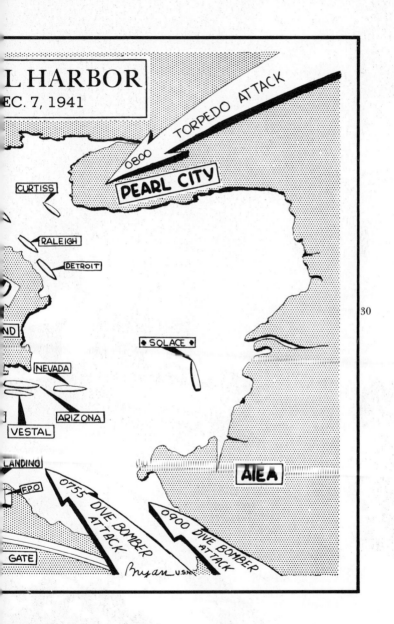

L HARBOR
EC. 7, 1941

TORPEDO ATTACK
0800
PEARL CITY

CURTISS

RALEIGH

DETROIT

30

ND

SOLACE

NEVADA

ARIZONA

VESTAL

LANDING

FPO

0755 DIVE BOMBER ATTACK

0900 DIVE BOMBER ATTACK

GATE

AIEA

Bryan USN

32   33

34

water as they made their drops. They screamed
overhead and away.

Her decks rocked as the *Utah* took two
thunderous hits. The old ship shuddered, and Van
knew that the hits were deadly. He had a fluttery,
weak feeling in his stomach as the ship started to
list and he realized she was going down.

Soon the abandon-ship order was being
bellowed. Van was on his way over the side when
he saw the man who had awakened him that
morning, sliding down a mooring cable. While he
was watching his friend, for only a few seconds,
another plane came in, its machine guns spitting.

The bullets ripped up his shipmate's side,
tearing off one arm and most of his head.

Even so, Van said, his friend clung to the
line for what seemed a long time. Then he let go,
as if reluctantly, and slipped down into the water.

At home, Al Sharkay shook me awake.

My first feeling was one of irritation. But
he said something strange was happening at Pearl,
and I'd better get up. His face was serious and his
manner disturbed, so I yanked on some clothes and
stumbled into the living room. Web Edwards, the
"Hawaii Calls" announcer, was on the air, his voice
tense. He kept repeating, "This is *no* drill. Pearl
Harbor is under attack. This is *no drill.* This is the
real McCoy."

Sharkay and I looked at each other. Without speaking we went outdoors and, far off over
the harbor area, saw a column of dark smoke rising
high. Specks darted about in the sky, looking like
gnats from our distance. Sharkay said he thought

we should get out there, and at almost the same moment Web Edwards announced that all Pearl Harbor workers should report immediately for duty. The neighborhood was quiet. No cars or people were moving about, not even children were playing.

While moving along Kapiolani Boulevard and across downtown Honolulu, we felt we were driving through any other Sunday, past a few solitary walkers, silent office buildings, and in sparse traffic. I remember thinking: Most people are still asleep. They should be awakened and told . . .

But our talk, the little we thought to do, was groping, uncertain, a wondering aloud. Maybe this wasn't really true. Maybe it was a crazy mistake by the air corps, or a special big army drill. Or perhaps a surprise exercise had been ordered, just to shock people into realizing that Hawaii *could* be attacked.

We drove fast over Keehi Lagoon bridge and past the old houses in Damon Tract. The dwellings themselves were peacefully silent, but on the highway through the cane fields more cars were speeding toward Pearl Harbor. As we neared Hickam Field and Pearl, we heard great booming and could see clouds of smoke rising high above the treetops ahead. By this time Sharkay and I had stopped talking, were only staring ahead, amazed and confused.

Cars were jammed up at the main gate. We pulled over to the side of the road, parked, and walked the rest of the way. Half-dressed marines, waving rifles with fixed bayonets, were herding men in by the dozens. I got separated

from Sharkay, and hopped aboard an open truck
with other arrivals. A whistling sound came from
the direction of the submarine base and a plane
flew over, low, less than a hundred feet above our
heads. We could see the red suns on its wings and
the head of the goggled pilot. The marines lifted
their rifles and fired wildly. The plane's guns
clattered briefly, digging up pieces of road and clods
of dirt, then bulleted on over Hickam. Oddly, in
the moment of quiet that followed, someone laughed.

I think it was then that I began to believe.

The truck dropped me off at the new
.shipfitters' shop. Across the road, along the docks
of the repair basin, men were dashing about on the
decks of the *Honolulu, San Francisco* and *St. Louis.*
There was similar activity around the *New Orleans,
Sacramento* and *Rigel,* and on smaller craft like
the *Ramapo* and the *Swan,* the latter drawn up dry
on the marine railway. Staccato anti-aircraft guns
fired. Past the roof of the machine shop dark smoke
blossomed, but the size of the big building barred
a view of what was happening in the outer harbor.

I stood rooted for many moments,
realizing at last that this was no mistake, no drill,
but something terribly real. Then suddenly, a
marine, crouched beside the building, was scream-
ing at me. "Get under cover, you dumb bastard!"
He shocked me into movement and I dashed inside
the shop. Its spaciousness seemed snug and safe
after the threats outside. Only about a dozen men
were there, and Dave Melville, my boss, was one.
Out of habit, I went to punch the time clock, and
Dave said, "Never mind that, Eddie, for Christ's

sake. Go over to Ten-Ten Dock and do what you can to help."

I eased out through the smaller opening in the big front door. More marines were outside, hugging the sides of the building. They clutched rifles and stared skyward. One snarled at me to get under cover, but the only way to get to Ten-Ten was to cross the roadway. The best way was to take a shortcut through the machine shop. So I ran across and ducked inside. Walking through it, I passed men standing beside their lathes and other kinds of machines. They were not working, only standing there, their faces pale and full of wondering. I thought of taking a minute to see if any of my friends were around, but decided I'd better do as I'd been told. The shop fronted on the long pier, facing Ford Island across the narrow waters. I walked through the front door and was stunned by what I saw.

It was like looking into Hell on a sunshiny day.

Each of the great battleships, so strong, clean and powerful yesterday, was in agony, tortured in an inferno of orange flame and vile smoke. Only the cage-like top sections of the masts on the *West Virginia* and *Tennessee* were visible through the roiling filth. The *California* looked half-sunk, listing on one side in snapping fires. The *Arizona* was almost completely hidden. Her superstructure tilted at a crazy angle amid oily clouds rising like thick black cauliflowers. The *Oklahoma* had rolled completely over. With her long bottom showing above water, she looked like an immense floating sausage. Tiny figures clustered on the higher places. Others were sliding down the rounded sides into the water.

Small boats moved back and forth on the edges of this fury, going in where tiny heads bobbed in the oily water or doll-like figures spilled over sides of broken ships. Muffled explosions belched and more flames lashed up as fires ignited fuel and ammunition stowages. The bursts were ghastly, vomiting pieces of the ships, and God only knew what else, into the air.

To me, the strangest thing of all was the awful clarity with which I was viewing the scene, this incredible carnage in a tropic morning. I had to tell myself that I was truly alive and awake and that this horror was real, not a bad dream—the water afire, the jarring, sickening explosions, and the small boats stark against the churning smoke and tongues of flame. All these abominations were utterly, terribly clear to my eyes, but my mind could not believe that this catastrophe was actually happening.

Close by, at dockside, the cruiser *Helena* had been hit and was listing. The minelayer *Oglala*, moored outboard, was being pulled away by tugs. Somehow I knew the *Oglala* was slowly sinking. I could *feel* as much as see it happening. Aboard the *Helena*, men darted about on the decks. Others were on the pier, waving arms and shouting. Suddenly I found myself in a line of men passing shells aboard. I remember a feeling of relief at doing something. But soon the chore was over, the line broke up, the others disappeared, and I was left alone. I felt useless, weak, insignificant. I looked for familiar faces to share a few words with, but none were near. For a chilling moment I had the thought that someone might shoot me, for loafing about so stupidly at such a devastating time. I started down Ten-Ten dock thinking: *There must be something I can do. Or perhaps someone will tell me what to do* . . . I half ran, as if on some important errand, then saw a boat coming across from the battleships. *They might need help,* I thought. *No one's on the dock to take their lines.* I was waiting when she came in, a launch filled with dark figures. The coxwain brought her bumping against the piling and someone threw me a line. I lashed it around a chock as best I could, tying knot upon knot, until a voice cried, "Hurry up for Christ's sake!" That was the coxswain, holding a stern line. I had forgotten there were two. He threw it, slithery with oil and hard to manage. But I hung on and secured that one too, knowing my technique was amateurish and wrong, but that the rope would hold.

The men started climbing ashore. Some were in mucky fouled denims, others wore whites soaked and shining with oil. All reeked of oil and smoke. A few talked and cursed, making little sense. Others were quiet, many had bloodless faces, their eyes in a glaze of shock. Five or six had to be helped ashore very carefully. One man screamed with every movement; his legs were rubbery and dangling uselessly. It took a long time to ease him up and I remember thinking how awful it would be if we dropped him in the harbor. He was covered with oil and difficult to hold.

The hardest job was lifting those wounded who were lying on the launch's deck. Two or three were quite still. A few others made weak movements, or clutching motions. They were dead weights when lifted, and the launch's sides dipped low in our struggles to raise them to the dock. I helped carry two over to an open area in front of the machine shop. I knew that one was dead. He was utterly limp, and his head rolled from side to side against my chest. I shall never forget the feel of that man. And I could tell from the eyes of the sailor helping me that he too, knew his shipmate was gone. We put the boy down gently among the wounded lying by the side of the road.

Now a few other boats were coming in from the chaos along Ford Island. The new arrivals stood on the long dock, dazed, staring back across the water. The battleships were still being eaten by fires and enshrouded in billowing, coal-black smoke. Sometimes breezes cleared air spaces for a few seconds, and we could see parts of the ships in a bluish gloom.

Soon, the boat I had helped was heading out, straight back into that Hell. The coxswain looked small, his legs apart on the stern as he held the tiller under his arm. He also looked very brave. The launch tossed up a grayish wake. Beyond it, brutal flowers of flame and smoke rose from the buckling ships.

Far away and high above, the Waianae Mountains slept on in their massive beauty, unmoved, untouched, as if nothing had happened.

I found a bucket and a faucet and I brought water. It seemed to be a useful thing to do.

Soon, a row of men lay in the area between the crane tracks and the machine shop. Some were dead, their faces covered with caps or bits of clothing. Others stirred, and their friends crouched close, talking and urging them over and over again to take it easy. I offered my cigarets and the pack disappeared in a minute. One young sailor was sitting by himself, sobbing beyond control. He kept pointing across the channel, trying to get his words out, but only choking sounds came.

Planes were still visible, high up, moving well above the shrapnel puffs. We could hear big and little guns thudding and rattling from Ford Island and Middle Loch ahead of us, and from the drydock nearby and the repair basin behind. Trucks and cars began arriving and we who were unhurt helped the wounded men into the vehicles. Again, after that, I had nothing to do for awhile. I had time then to consider how frightened I was, how drenched in fear, as I stood thinking: *Those bastards are coming back and next time I will be killed. We will all be killed. How can men do this to one another?* I felt sickened, helpless, useless. A foreign part of me was moving and walking through all this misery and horror. The part I was aware of was staring, wondering and tense. I started for Drydock One with the thought: *That's where my job is, that's where I should be.*

One big ship was in the stream of East Loch—the battleship *Nevada,* obviously trying to get out of the harbor. She too had been badly hit. Her bow was down, fire flickered and smoke trailed her decks. But she was underway, a fine and gallant sight. I remember saying to myself: *Thank God, there's at least one left.*

LESS THAN AN HOUR, and now it was history.

Fuchida studied the holocaust below.

He and his first-wave planes were soon nearing the return-point in fuel time. Other pilots were departing, their work done, but as commander he was charged with bringing back a complete report. Visibility was difficult through the smoke from fires below, but he continued to circle until his time ran to the danger point.

The second wave of planes arrived from the carriers at 8:40. Eighty were Val dive-bombers, fifty, level bombers, and thirty-six, protective fighters. The job of the Vals was to strike vessels only damaged by the first wave or not yet hit. The Zero fighters were able to fly free, pouncing and strafing at their choice, without any air opposition at all.

The mission was clear, and the second wave needed no instructions from Fuchida. He banked his aircraft for a final look around. It was not going to be as easy for the new arrivals. Now the Americans were furiously aroused, and the sky was freckled with anti-aircraft explosions. Obviously, every available gun on ship and ashore was spitting fire aloft.

The second wave dispersed on its deadly errands. The commander of the Val squadrons began guiding his men down into the mouths of American guns. Fuchida's time had run out. He started back to the waiting carriers, pausing only long enough to round up a few Zeros wandering about aimlessly. Diversionary flights planned earlier to deceive pursuing Americans were not necessary, he decided. Today, the air was Japanese. He headed straight for home. Admiral Nagumo, realizing that minutes and miles would be precious to the fliers, had moved the task force forty miles nearer to Oahu.

In Washington the time was two o'clock in the afternoon.

A stunned secretary of state, Cordell Hull, heard the news of the attack from President Roosevelt and hung up his telephone.

Beyond Hull's office door, Ambassadors Nomura and Kurusu waited, each wearing spectacles, a sedate suit and muted tie. Hull knew what they brought to him. At 8 o'clock that morning the last section of a fourteen-part message from Tokyo to the two ambassadors had been decoded by MAGIC. Now they were delivering the memorandum. It was a recapitulation of Japanese-American negotiations and a reaffirmation of Japan's objections. The paragraphs were accusatory and belligerent, stating among other things that it was "obviously the intention of the American government to conspire with Great Britain and other countries to obstruct Japan's efforts toward the establishment of peace through the creation of a New Order in East Asia and especially to preserve Anglo-American rights by keeping Japan and China at war." The closing statement, in diplomatic terms, was chilling in finality:

"The Japanese Government regrets to have to notify the American Government that in view of the attitude of the American Government it cannot but consider that it is impossible to reach an agreement through further negotiations."

Nomura and Kurusu had been instructed to deliver the memorandum at 1 p.m. But problems with decoding the message and typing the translation had delayed them. They handed the message to Hull at 2:30, with apologies for their tardiness. The attack had been going on for well over an hour.

Seething under his surface coolness, Hull made a pretense of reading the paper. Then he told the Japanese that in all his fifty years of public service he had never read a document that was more crowded with falsehoods and distortions—"Falsehoods and distortions on a scale so huge that I never imagined until today that any government on this planet was capable of uttering them."

The shaken, frozen-faced ambassadors were led away into internment. To his dying day each man swore that on December 7th, 1941, he knew nothing about an attack on Pearl Harbor.

Fuchida and the first wave of attack planes began touching down on their carriers at 10 o'clock. High seas and capricious winds made landings difficult. By noon, aircraft of the second wave were arriving.

There had been some losses in bombers and fighters shot down; others, radioing banzai as they ran out of fuel, had plummeted into the sea. Twenty-nine planes in all. A small sacrifice for the enormous success achieved.

Elation and activity were feverish aboard the Japanese ships. As the planes landed they were immediately refueled and rearmed. Minoru Genda wanted to send the squadrons to seek out and engage the American aircraft carriers. Mitsuo Fuchida was equally eager to lead them back to Oahu. He urged Admiral Nagumo to permit his men to strike again. Nagumo thought about it.

Fuchida argued: Many targets at Pearl Harbor were still untouched; the machine shop and other repair facilities were undamaged; millions of gallons of fuel oil stored aboveground were unharmed; American submarines had not been hit.

Nagumo thought more about it. He might endanger a rendezvous that had been set for refueling his ships. The American carriers might cause fatal wounds to some of his carriers if they were found. A steel-starved Japan could not afford to lose a single vessel. And his mission had been accomplished; the U.S. Pacific Fleet lay in ruins.

"We may conclude that anticipated results have been achieved," he said. He ordered his task force to sail back to Japan. At 1:30 that Sunday afternoon they were underway.

Fuchida was so angry that he scarcely spoke to the admiral all the way home.

When the second-wave planes came in they appeared as if from out of nowhere, even soundless at first.

They darted like angry birds at the *Nevada,* hitting her again and again. From a distance she seemed to shiver and shrug, but miraculously kept moving. Moments later racking detonations came from the nearby drydock area. Concussions followed, pulsing blasts of warm wind.

I wanted desperately to hide, to crawl under something, anything, but there was no place to go. I realized that those last hits must have been made on the *Pennsylvania, Cassin,* or *Downes*— perhaps on all three. A crane moving beside the drydock stopped. Flames leaped out of the big sunken basin and smoke whorled up. I thought for a moment about the chief doing his Christmas cards there, only the night before. I kept moving toward the drydock. I didn't want to go, but could think of nothing else to do. Then the destroyer *Shaw* was hit, out on the floating drydock.

The eruption was monstrous, appalling. The ship appeared to disintegrate into a million pieces, becoming a gargantuan fireball. The blast sent scraps twisting and flying in all directions, for thousands of feet, in great slow-motion arcs trailing streamers of smoke. I was probably a quarter of a mile away, yet one of the pieces fell at my feet. I picked it up, a curl of steel ripped clean and shiny, handball-sized. I thought of keeping it as a souvenir; it would have made a conversation-piece as a paperweight. Then I threw it away.

A truck raced up and an elderly man got out and asked me for help. His flatbed was covered with cans and we worked for about ten minutes unloading and placing them by the roadside. While we labored, there was another explosion in the drydock. But we kept working, not speaking. Then he drove the truck away and I was alone again. To this day I have no idea what was in those cans or why we unloaded them.

Approaching the drydock again I could see that the *Pennsylvania* was sitting high and straight, but with thick smoke rising from amidships. In front, the superstructure of the *Downes* was erect, but the *Cassin* alongside had toppled over, her topside crushed against her sister ship. Looking down into the drydock brought another shock. Someone had ordered it flooded for safety and the three ships sat in a rising pool of thick black oil. Debris of every description seemed to be glued upon the gummy surface: pieces of scaffolding, life preservers, pennants, scraps of clothing and containers. It was a loathsome mess, the *Cassin* on her side almost completely under, the *Downes,* nearly torn in two with a great gaping hole amidships where a bomb had taken the bridge. Crewmen dashed over the *Pennsylvania*'s decks. Men everywhere played streams of water on fires, soaking decks and explosive places where fire threatened, raising clouds of pallid steam.

I joined one of the gangs at dockside. Tai Sing Loo, a stubby Chinese who wore a varnished straw safari helmet and was known to all of us as a character, bustled about, giving orders. I recall thinking: *He is the yard photographer and suddenly he is giving us orders.* But Loo was no longer just a Character. He had taken charge and his instructions made sense. We obeyed without question, finding and placing planks to protect water lines, clearing tracks for the cranes, hauling hoses, moving debris, and servicing trucks. Crewmen carried blanket-covered bodies off the *Pennsylvania.* Others stared down at the tangled embrace of the *Cassin* and *Downes.* Time did not move. We felt best when we were doing something, anything.

My memories of the hours that followed in that morning are tossed and tumbled, without chronology, covering acts ranging from furious work to panicky pauses.

We did what we were told to do, or thought needed doing, then stared at each other, or again and again at the carnage in the harbor. When we worked we did so with relief because we didn't have to look at each other, or at the destruction around us, or spend thought upon wondering when they were coming back. It seemed useless to hope that the Japanese would not return.

We didn't talk very much. Almost all the men in the drydock area were strangers to each other or only slightly familiar faces brought together by chance. Other than Tai Sing Loo and a rigger or two I barely knew any of the others. Dave Melville appeared briefly, but navy officers had taken over and he soon went elsewhere. Each of us worked quite alone with his thoughts. Communications were terse and gruff, mostly exclamations of anger and impatience. We could see cars and trucks scurrying to the small hospital beyond the yawning hole of the new Number Two Drydock. Across the harbor several battleships were obscured in fire and smoke for quite a while. The *Oglala* was on her side along Ten-Ten Dock. The *Nevada* was aground near the harbor entrance. The *Pennsylvania*'s guns pointed skyward and her decks bustled with activity.

A pall of haze hung over the whole scene. Immense black clouds rolled up from the broken *Arizona* long after fires elsewhere had been extinguished. Ugly smoke rose from hangars on Ford Island.

Often there were silences, as the shouts, hammerings and hissings died down for long moments. These pauses seemed charged with an intolerable dread, their quiet creating a sound ominous in itself. In these moments we would look up. But the sky remained empty of planes.

154

I was back at the shipfitters' shop early in the afternoon.

Other workers had straggled in and their stories were excited and jumbled. Rumors flew about like sparrows. We listened because it was urgent to listen, to talk about something, our physical nearness to one another was not enough.

Men were saying that there were saboteurs in the shipyard; that paratroopers had landed in nearby canefields, and enemy troops were coming ashore at Waikiki and Honolulu; that Oahu's drinking water had been poisoned—even that the United States had surrendered Hawaii to Japan. This last rumor we refused to believe, and none of the stories turned out to have even a remote acquaintance with the truth.

Our bosses and navy officers were talking gravely in a group behind the glass windows of the shop office. We waited. Apparently they decided that some workers should be sent home, to return later for all-night standby. The cheerless presumption was that all the shipyard's workers wouldn't be killed if the Japanese attacked again.

Dave Melville passed on the instructions; his gang was among those chosen to get out. We asked if we had a choice about staying. Dave said no, for us to leave and get some rest. There would be plenty to do when we came back. His tone couldn't disguise his vagueness.

Like the others, I had mixed feelings about leaving. Despite the raw cold fear of dying, I also detected a recognizable urge to stay, to be with men I knew. Outside, the guns on the ships had long been quiet. But had the Japanese left for good or only withdrawn for awhile? No one knew. In the hours since the second wave flew off, several ships had been able to clear the harbor. There were empty spaces now where the *St. Louis*, *Sacramento* and *New Orleans* had been docked. The *Honolulu* and *Rigel* were still at pierside, and the *Swan* remained perched on the marine railway.

I thumbed a ride out of Pearl and dropped off in Waikiki, hoping I'd find friends there.

Waikiki was not Waikiki that afternoon. The sleepiness was gone, the air charged with shock and fear.

Knots of people were strung along Kalakaua Avenue, in front of the Tavern and the drugstore, under the banyan tree. The groups buzzed with news and rumors: the United States had declared war; there would be strict blackout that night; special police were being signed up; Hawaii would be placed under martial law; bombs had fallen on the city and civilians had been killed. And often, through all the talk, the questions were repeated: would the Japanese come back? Was this only a time of waiting before an invasion? Some people talked about getting guns, wondering aloud what to do, where to go . . .

Wives of marines and navy men moved from group to group, asking questions of anyone who had been at Pearl. One pretty young woman said her husband was assigned to the *Arizona*. She heard it had been hit. Her lips trembled. What had happened? Was it bad? Were the men all right? I remember telling her I didn't know, then getting away as gracefully as I could. The *Arizona* was a bomb-ripped corpse. Anyone who had seen it knew that few of her men had survived, if any.

I walked to the cottages of friends. All were empty, their occupants probably still at the shipyard. In one of the silent houses I stretched on a couch, but couldn't rest. It was too quiet, being alone was grim, the memories imprinted on my mind during those searing morning hours stayed with me. I had brought all of them back to the cool room in Waikiki. The flames, faces and explosions would not leave me. I lay there realizing I was unable to accept what had happened. I had seen, heard and felt a tragedy beyond absorbing, and it was inconceivable to me still. Surely, I promised myself, when I go back this evening, Pearl Harbor will be calm and peaceful again, just as it was yesterday.

My thoughts raced, fragmented, rarely finished. I should telephone my parents, I told myself, to let them know I'm all right. But telephone service to the mainland had been cut off to civilians. I wondered about my brother who loved racing cars, and then about the other, in the army in Georgia, and went on to my sister, at home in Massachusetts. I wondered about the night and what it would bring. I felt an aloneness never known before, a sundering from friends, books, belongings. Family faces suddenly became sharp and clear. Our years of depression poorness didn't seem sad at all. I wanted very much to see them again, and solemnly wondered if I ever would.

The quiet of the room became eerie. Not a voice murmured or a footstep sounded in the lanes outside. I got up and went back to the beach, walking along the Kuhio seawall, avoiding the gatherings in the area around the Tavern. The cribbage players clustered together still, although

their games were forgotten. The old men chattered
excitedly and, listening, I realized they were not
displeased by what had happened. Their conversation was outraged and angry on the surface,
but it betrayed unspoken hopes: conceivably now
they might be recalled to service, go home again
to ships and barracks, to uniforms and duty.
I thought of how the dazed young men at Pearl
looked by comparison.

I found a bench all for myself and stared at
the sea, thinking, God only knew what was out
there. The horizon's line was blue-black, the sun
far into its drop. Back-lighting turned the tops of
the combers into a milky blue. There was something unusual about the scene, something
disturbing. Then I realized the difference; no one
was riding in the surf or strolling along the sand.

Soon it was time for me to go back to Pearl.
I went to the drugstore corner, knowing that
there I'd find a ride.

In late afternoon we headed back for Pearl in
Jimmy Jones's car. Jimmy was my age, we had
worked together frequently, and were friends.
Happy Peura, a rigger and older man, rode with us,
along with a boy named Red King. Red was a
local haole, gangling, bedaubed with freckles
and still in his teens. He was accomplished in the
use of island pidgin and often kept us laughing
while explaining expressions like "Why you no stop
come stay dis place?" But laughter did not go
along with us on this trip. Indeed, we said very
little. Happy hugged a pint jug and sipped at
it morosely.

Jimmy's wife had retreated to her mother's house after a squabble a few days before. Now he wanted to see her. On the way through town he found the house and went in. He was gone for only a few minutes and when the door opened his wife was weeping. They held each other for a long time. When he came back to the car no one said a word. I remember wishing that I had someone to say goodbye to.

Dusk was gathering and a complete blackout had been ordered. Earlier, orders had been broadcast that any cars authorized to travel must have their headlights painted blue at the main police station. There was a long line of cars at the Bethel Street side. Finally our turn came and the cops slapped paint on the lights, sloshing blue over the car's front. Jimmy was quite incensed; he was a scrupulously neat man and fussy-proud of his car's appearance.

We headed out Dillingham Boulevard as dark descended. Except for an occasional army or police vehicle, Honolulu seemed to be abandoned. We saw no pedestrians, only buildings looking empty, with windows staring vacantly. Farther out on the highway we met more traffic coming our way, the blue lights on the cars like monster's eyes in the twilight. Several times we were stopped by fidgety soldiers or police who asked our destination and demanded identification. At the Pearl Harbor gate, surly marines, looking older now, checked our badges and faces carefully. Their eyes were red-rimmed, their uniforms smudged and disheveled.

Inside, the yard vibrated with bustle and tension.

Many figures moved about on the unlighted docks and ships. Happy left us to join his fellow riggers. Jimmy, Red, and I went into the ship-fitters' shop. We sat in that immense barn, wondering what we were to do and what might happen as night fell. Crane cabs overhead were empty, lines and hooks dangling. Other scattered men and the big machines on the shop floor were only dim shapes in the deepening light. It was strange not to hear good-natured cries, or the big brakes and shears clanking. Blued flashlights of our bosses, quartermen and leadingmen, jerked dulled arrows of light over the long floor. We workers were told we'd have no light. Flashlights were forbidden and if we so much as struck a match we would be shot, no questions, no delay, and this was no bullshit. The order was for an absolute blackout, and the marines were edgy and angry. No one said the words, but we knew everyone was thinking that the Japanese would be coming back.

The waiting continued. We shuffled about uneasily or huddled in small gatherings. For the most part it was quiet outside, the ships and harbor a world hung in apprehension. But now and then a ship or shore station would test its guns and our nerves would scream with their bursts. When the brief rattles ended you could hear sighs of relief all around.

After dark an unseen Samaritan brought in a big urn of strong coffee and we gulped it down gratefully. Coffee had never tasted better. Soon, we tried to sleep, stretching out on tool boxes or the wooden blocks of the flooring. But sleep was impossible. So we made conversation, exchanging scraps of news: two Japanese midget subs had been sunk in the harbor; the *Utah* was under, and the *Nevada* beached at Waipio Point so she wouldn't block the harbor's entrance. The *California* and *West Virginia* were very badly hit; the *Shaw's* bow had been blown away, and the tug, *Sotoyomo,* had sunk behind her. There was no damage to the submarine base and the carriers had been at sea.

On the far side of Ford Island, the *Raleigh* had been hit critically, but the *Detroit* was untouched. Back on Battleship Row, the *Maryland* had been one of the luckier survivors. Being inboard of the capsized *Oklahoma,* she had taken only a bruising. But the *Tennessee* had been severely damaged, even though she was moored inland of the sunken *West Virginia.* When the *Arizona* was mentioned, we could only shake our heads. She was a shambles, still burning.

Men were still trapped inside the capsized *Oklahoma.* Knocking signals from the entombed sailors could be heard, and chippers from our shop were trying frantically to free them, no one knew how many. At first, the rescuers had tried to cut through the hull plates with acetylene torches. But this was too dangerous, because the flame might ignite gases or oil and kill those who were still alive. Now it was being done the slow, hard, safe way, cutting through the thick plates with air-driven chisels, a few inches at a time.

About 8 o'clock a few of the chippers came back to the shop. They stood by the office doors, towels draped around their necks, drinking coffee and conferring with the bosses. The burly crew looked like a muster of wrestlers. I listened, standing close beside them. They were saying how awful it was to hear the knocking of the trapped men. "There are guys *dying* in there who still don't know what the hell happened," one said.

The chippers didn't linger long. They were exhausted, but anxious to get back to work. When they left we envied them. At least they were doing something. For the rest of us, there was only waiting.

Dave Melville found me in the dark. He told me to take my helper and go up to the mold loft. "Richards is the boss," he said. "He'll tell you what to do."

My helper was one of about a dozen Chinese lads assigned to our shop on some sort of training program to help Chiang Kai-shek's China. They were bright and eager lads but without a language in common, the training idea was doomed. I beckoned my boy out from a huddle of his chums near a pile of steel, and could see the whites of his eyes, even in the gloom. We felt our way up the stairwell. It was very dark, but I preferred fumbling up stairs to the vague threat of being imprisoned in an elevator if something happened. Every minute seemed to be swollen with disaster.

When we reached the loft we found other shipfitters there with their helpers: Richards, a bespectacled chain-chewer of cigars, and Enoch Spencer, almost pure Hawaiian, with a striking aristocratic face. Enoch was friendly and gentle, but not a talker. The third man was Sammy Morgan, the chubby Scot. I was happy to see Sammy. Some men put out a warming glow and Sammy was such a one.

All were shadowy figures, standing or sitting on the floor against the wall. The loft reminded me of a huge, dark vacuum. Richards suggested that we take turns patrolling the vacant expanse because there was a possibility of paratroopers or saboteurs coming in during the night. We were to listen for noises on the roof above our heads, and stay alert for suspicious movements anywhere. I would make the check first, he told me, going down one side of the long room then coming back along the other.

To me the place seemed acres of murky threat. A row of windows on the repair basin side overlooked the blurred ships in their berths among the piers. I could neither see nor hear movement outside, but I knew very well that thousands of men were down there, under cover, taut, scared and waiting, as we were. Mine was a lonely patrol, despite the nearness of the others. The only sounds came from the scratch of my footsteps or a crackling as I stepped on pieces of the flat white wood the loft men used for cutting templates. The weird shapes lay scattered about, like bleached bones in a cave.

When I returned to my gang, Richards was munching his cigar and talking about a small movie theater he owned back home in the states. Enoch Spencer and all the helpers were saying nothing. Sammy Morgan volunteered a wisecrack now and then and chuckled a great deal. He was in fine spirits, I thought, then knew why when a waft of his breath floated my way. When Richards's story trailed to an end, Sammy started a yarn about his service in the British army during World War I, and a special night when he'd been sent to dig a tunnel toward the German lines.

"I heerd this scratchin' and knew it could only be one thing. Then all of a sudden the dirt came down and there was this Jerry soljer. Nice as you please, there he was, starin' at me."

He paused. I asked what happened next.

"Why I killed the bahstud with me shovel," Sammy said pleasantly.

There was a humming sound overhead. The roar that followed was skull-splitting. Every gun at Pearl Harbor raged into action. Tens of thousands of tracers streaked skyward from every direction, making a tent of fire. An explosion followed, almost over our heads, and the roof rumbled with the concussion. A plane had been hit. We saw it, flaming down toward Ford Island.

The big building vibrated and rattled like a flimsy tin box. Guns outside were spitting like a thousand Roman candles. I fell to the floor, fervently wishing I could burrow beneath the planks. I had never known such helpless fear. Always before there had been a wisp of hope in my fear, whether in fire, or falling or drowning. But this was a fear that froze; there was no thought or control in it, only a pure and paralyzing terror.

I prayed, "Hail Mary, full of grace . . ." and "Jesus, Mary and Joseph, pray for us sinners . . ." Prayers I had not said for a long time. My fingers hurt from clutching the floor. Everyone else was flattened too. Except Sammy Morgan. Outlined in flashings beyond the windows, he leaned on one elbow, viewing whatever was happening out there, incredibly casual.

The firing stopped. The sudden silence was enormous. No one spoke for long moments.

"Now's a good time, if you owe any Japanese any money, to tell them to go fook themselves," said Sammy.

The aircraft shot down that night were our own, we later learned. Three of them, trying to get in from the *Enterprise* in the blackout. By a miracle all the pilots escaped.

After that the quiet settled in again. Nerves tingled and hours crawled. We ran out of talk. Richards set up turns for patrols again and we took our solitary walks to return, sit, and wait. And the waiting went on.

I ached for sleep, for its sweet escape, but could not accept the blessing. If I wanted to smoke a cigaret, I had to go into the washroom and hang pieces of clothing over the windows. Once, when I lighted up, I was startled to see Enoch Spencer. His brown Hawaiian face was grave in the flare from the match.

"What do you think?" he asked after a few moments.

I told him I didn't know what to think. I had no mechanism for thinking. I was just scared cold. Perhaps those planes were scouts, sent before the big flights of Japanese came back. The next attack would be the end for us all.

Enoch was silent. Then he said softly, "God has done this. He is doing this to punish us."

I was taken aback, having no answer to such a message. I think I mumbled something about His having to punish them too.

"This is only the beginning," Enoch went on. "I think God is punishing the world, all the world."

That ended our conversation. We merely

stood there. Soon Enoch left. When I finished my cigaret I went back into the loft and sat down again to wait.

I thought of many things: of God and what he gave us; of what it would be like to die; and of a girl I had loved once upon a time. I thought of my brothers, and my mother, father and sister, in their little house outside Lowell, worrying about me. It would be cold in New England now, with the first thin ice crusting the streams, the elms and maples leafless and stark. I wished I could let them know that I was still alive. I regretted not writing more often . . . And I thought of the year past in Hawaii, the friends I'd made and good times we'd had, recognizing them now as priceless.

That night was an endlessness, a fitful journey in and out of half-sleep from which I awoke startled, with eyes smarting and limbs cramped. When I took my turns around the loft, the ships and docks below were almost formless, completely silent. They showed no signs of life, but many men were there, some huddled under cranes or piles of steel and lumber, others beside their guns. And those who died were there too, not knowing why they had died, and those still trapped who were going to die, not knowing why. And beyond, were the people in Honolulu, in the valleys, on the neighbor islands, hiding, with their doors closed and lights turned off, waiting and frightened. All Hawaii lay in darkness, save that the still burning *Arizona*, a smoldering pyre, was like a beacon fire for Oahu.

Hours later someone gave me an orange. I

peeled it, inhaling its burst of sweet fragrance,
tasting its tart and cleansing sting.

Finally morning came, its first gray smear-
ings seen through the loft's windows. Slowly,
color returned to the world. Men raised their voices
and sounds of activity lifted up from the repair
basin. But sitting up there, listening, I knew that
a most special year was ended, and a memorable
time for me, and that mornings would never be
quite the same again.

Two or three days later I went aboard the
Downes.

The ships in Drydock One still rested
ignominiously in a hideous pool of oil and debris.
I walked across a teetering gangplank to the
destroyer's deck, terrified of falling into the black
pond.

The *Downes's* charthouse was demolished,
and a great, ragged hole opened aft of its remnants.
The *Cassin*, alongside, broken and mangled, leaned
against her sister ship. I moved forward gingerly
on decks covered with slippery oil. Cables,
piping, and wiring lay twisted underfoot or drooped
from overhead. Doors hung crazily and glass
from shattered ports was strewn everywhere.
Galley stoves were overturned, blackened and
crumpled pots and pans lay where they had
been tossed.

In what remained of the crews' quarters,
oil dripped from above in a slow, even rhythm.
The smell was sickening. In the area where the
chief and I had sat as he addressed his Christmas

cards, the decking had buckled and heat of the fires had crumpled bulkheads and other heavy plates like so much cardboard. I regretted my coming back.

An object caught my eye. A book, its covers and outside pages burned away. What remained was soaked, almost to a pulp. I opened it. A Bible. And the first legible words I read were from the book of Ezekiel:
"They walked not in my statutes and they despised my judgements, which if a man do he shall even live in them; and my sabbaths they greatly polluted. Then I said I would pour out my fury, to consume them."

LIST OF ILLUSTRATIONS

(Most of the photographs reproduced in this book were taken in 1941; a few, however, are from earlier or later years. The following abbreviations have been used in giving photographic credits:

RVD-RJB **Ray Jerome Baker photographs from the Robert E. Van Dyke Collection of Hawaiiana.**
USN **United States Navy.**
USNO **Official United States Navy Photo.)**

Honolulu and Pearl Harbor. RVD-RJB

12   Waikiki Tavern (1941). RVD-RJB
13   Honolulu firemen, showing musical, dancing,
      and singing skills (1941). RVD-RJB
14   Waikiki Beach (1941). RVD-RJB
15   On the town (1941). RVD-RJB
16   Ford Island, Pearl Harbor (1941). Battleship
      Row is at the right. USNO
17   Halekulani Hotel, Waikiki (*ca.* 1940). RVD-RJB
18   Upper Fort Street, downtown Honolulu (1941).
      RVD-RJB
19   King and Bishop Streets, downtown Honolulu
      (1941). RVD-RJB
20   Matson Line ship leaving Honolulu Harbor
      (1941). RVD-RJB
21   Bus to Pearl Harbor, about to leave from the
      depot on Hotel Street, downtown Honolulu
      (1941). RVD-RJB
22   Honolulu Harbor, looking northwest toward
      Pearl Harbor and the Waianae Mountains
      (1941). Courtesy of *Honolulu Magazine,* successor
      to *Paradise of the Pacific.*
23   Japanese model of Pearl Harbor, used in
      planning the attack. Photographer unknown.
24   Typical Honolulu market (*ca.* 1940). RVD-RJB
25   Youngsters garbed as Hawaiian nobility (date
      uncertain). Hawaii Visitors Bureau photograph.
26   Black Cat Cafe, Hotel Street, downtown
      Honolulu (1940). RVD-RJB
27   Herbalist in Honolulu's Chinatown (1941).
      RVD-RJB
28   A view of Diamond Head from the grounds of
      the Halekulani Hotel, Waikiki (?1945). George

꼭꼭**ᴋꌗꟼꌗ**

DAYS OF '41: PEARL HARBOR REMEMBERED

Consulting editor, Charles R. Temple (Honolulu). Book design and typography by Clemente Lagundimao (Honolulu). Cover design by Myles Tanaka (Honolulu). Manufactured under the supervision of John Weatherhill, Inc. (Tokyo). Composition by Innovative Media, Inc. (Honolulu). Printing by Kimmei Printing Company (Tokyo). Binding by the Makoto Binderies (Tokyo). Text set in Baskerville 10-point, with 2-point leading, and School-book Bold 8-point, with 4-point leading.

A Kapa Associates Publication